Reviewed
18/6/98

GARAVI GUJARAT GROUP
LIBRARY

12 JUN

D1333144

*Letters from India*

# Letters from India

QUENTIN CREWE

LONG BARN BOOKS

## To Nat

PUBLISHED BY
LONG BARN BOOKS

Ebrington, Gloucestershire GL55 6NW

First published 1998
1 3 5 7 9 10 8 6 4 2

Copyright © Quentin Crewe 1998

All rights reserved

Without limiting the rights under copyright reserved
above, no part of this publication may be reproduced, stored in
or introduced into a retrieval system, or transmitted, in any
form or by any means (electronic, mechanical, photocopying,
recording or otherwise) without prior written permission of both
the copyright owner and above publisher of this book.

Set in 10.75/13.5pt Monotype Sabon
Printed and bound by Redwood Books, Trowbridge, Wiltshire

ISBN 0 952 8285 8 8

# Prologue

At the end of 1991, I suddenly found myself homeless. For ten years, I had lived in an idyllic hamlet in Haute Provence that belonged to a friend. He had decided to live in India and to give the hamlet to his children. It seemed hardly fair that they should be encumbered with a permanent guest, however old a friend of their father. It was time for me to move on. The question was, where to?

There was a parlour game quality about the decision. Given the whole world to chose from, how does one decide? Outside Europe, the countries I have loved most are Kenya and Peru. The past fifteen years have ruined Kenya, making it an unsettled, even dangerous choice. The same is true of Peru, added to which the great altitudes do not suit my respiritory problems.

Much of the world suffers from similar unrest. Of course, there are beautiful places like Jamaica and Bali, but islands rapidly become claustrophobic. Morocco and Thailand, while amusing, do attract a narrow kind of expatriate.

My thoughts turned more and more towards India. Some five years before, I had spent six happy months living in Jaipur while researching a book. Furthermore I had friends in Delhi and Calcutta and now my recent host from France was building a house high in the South Indian hills of Kerala.

It happened that my twenty-two year old son Nat had given up his job. The idea of a trip to India appealed to him. We flew first to Nairobi, there confirming that I did not want to live in Kenya and then, on to Bombay.

The man who pushed my wheelchair when we got off the plane at Bombay was effusive. 'Welcome to India. You will be very happy, you are my friend.' He kept up a lively stream of chat and inquiry as we bowled along the corridors. 'Coming from?' This was not to ask where my flight had come from, but to ask where I lived. We established that and whether Nat, who was with me, was my son, how many other sons and daughters I had, how much my wheelchair had cost and endless other bits of information of varying degrees of intimacy. 'I will take you all over India and look after you and then you will take me back to your country.' To emphasise the warmth of our friendship he massaged my shoulders and patted my cheek.

By the time we arrived at the passport control, which he said he would get us through at exceptional speed, I felt we were ready to swear eternal friendship like two characters in an Italian opera.

The passport official took our documents. My friend announced that he must fetch something, but would be back in a moment. I never saw him again.

I could hardly take offence at this almost instant betrayal, for I had not been very forthcoming in answering all his questions. In my English way, I had not wanted to explain that I had come to India to look for somewhere to live and that for medical reasons, I had decided to leave Europe. It all seemed a bit emotional to go into at the end of a long journey.

What I had forgotten was that this is one of the charms of India, that people do not hesitate to discuss quite private matters on the slightest acquaintance and that they regard our reticence as stand-offish. It reveals, I think, a more genuine concern for others.

India is an atmosphere, a state of mind rather than a place. No two bits of India are the same, so it is no good saying India is hot or India is cold, or India is violent or India is peaceful, because any statement will be true about somewhere in India at any given moment.

It takes time to adjust to this atmosphere which, on the surface, appears familiar, in that so many people speak English, that all signs are in English, that so many relics of British rule remain. Yet underneath it is totally strange and confusing.

While so much may seem customary, nothing prepares one for the visual impact – the cascade of colour, the vibrant energy of the mass of people, the endless incident. A man bicycles past, a loudspeaker on his handlebars shrieking at one to buy lottery tickets. At a stall men are brewing tea, they put the tea, the milk and the sugar all in together, boil it and strain it through what looks like an old sock. It has an odd taste that grows on you.

A superb jacaranda tree, vivid with its rich flowers of pale violet, grows out of a thin grey, rubbish heap, the refuse of a society that has nothing to throw away. One sign reads, God Almighty Tailors; another Spittle, Urine

4

and Stools tested here. Two women in clashing fuchsia sarees, with brass pots on their heads, lean against a doorway, gossiping. An old Saddhu in spotless white, his long beard dividing into two wispy rivers of fluffiness, bows his head in greeting as he passes by. A group of mourners, chanting softly, carry shoulder-high on a wattle stretcher, a corpse wrapped simply in a shroud. A hundred little schoolgirls in brilliant yellow tunics rush in hesitant leaps across the road, followed by scores of blue-shirted schoolboys.

The traffic moves in a kind of dance. There is a vague principle that you keep to the left, but there is no need to be slavish about this. Overtaking is normal on blind corners and when you can see something coming towards you. The only thing is to be sure that all parties in any sort of tangle have an escape route of some kind, a few inches of verge, a narrow gap between two mammoth buses or, for pedestrians, a stone they can hop onto. Amazingly the cows and the goats that wander in the streets are absolutely conversant with the rules. Hooted at or flashed at, the cows sway with dignity and the goats skip crossly in just the direction you want them to go.

It works very well most of the time, but on any long day's journey one is sure to see the results of at least one dramatic crash.

We had planned to fly on the next day from Bombay. A friend had booked seats for us. The hotel had a travel agent in the lobby. It did not open in the morning till nine. Impossible to confirm our flights so late, they said. At the airport it was too late to buy tickets at one desk, we must go to another section. There they had gone for tea. And so it went on, with one obstacle after another. Julius, the man from the hotel who, without being asked, had come with us to help, smiled at each setback. Slowly, just in time, every hurdle was overcome. As always in India, with a little patience and the right guide, the impossible gets done. We were on our way to the first place where I might want to live.

Everyone, whether English or Indian, said, 'You must go to the Nilgiri Hills, you will love it there, it is just like England, or perhaps Scotland.'

As I had been recommended to find a different climate to live in, I was not too sure of the usefulness of this advice. I also had an uneasy recollection of what the explorer Sir Richard Burton had had to say about Ootacamund, when he was sent there as a young subaltern on sick leave from Bombay.

He had hated it and wrote that for most of the time it was shrouded in what might just as well have been a London fog that lifted very occasionally to reveal a thick Scottish mist, or words to that effect.

It proved to be a lot better than that. We drove for two-and-a-half hours in a taxi up more than 5,000 feet on a twisting, crowded road, marvelling at the clairvoyance of the driver, who would overtake on a hairpin bend, but somehow never came face to face with one of the countless lorries and buses that came swirling down the hill at thundering speed.

The road from Coimbatore, running at first through a thickly populated area, was thronged with every sort of lumbering vehicle, spewing out great clouds of black exhaust. In among them were bullock carts, pulled by bullocks with huge curving horns. The horns were painted in bright colours, sometimes both horns would be the same colour, but more often they were different – reds, blues and greens predominating. At the foot of the blue hills, we passed through coconut groves and crossed the railway that was literally to claw its way to Ootacamund on a line so steep that in places the train has to be ratchetted up the slope.

Then we climbed through a forest of soaring trees. Every so often, at a sharp corner, a stream fell down the hillside, like a silver rope, and monkeys played at the edge of the road, wary of the traffic, but hopeful of a dropped banana skin. At a larger stream, we stopped and men rushed to fill our bubbling radiator.

The air grew cooler and was filled now with the scent of eucalyptus and pine. The solid wall of the forest parted now and then to expose wide spaces of shrill emerald green – the tufted gardens of tea. All along the verges there were great bushes of lantana, covered in small flowers of mixed pink and yellow, pretty and enchanting until one smells them.

We were to stay with friends at Coonoor, a sort of poor man's Ootacamund. The British had a Staff College there and the tea gardens brought plenty of Europeans. It was, however, a working place, unlike Ooty with its packs of foxhounds and houses of absurd splendour.

The hillsides are sprinkled with houses built to remind the original owners of Surrey or Dumfries, often with Tudor features or classical pediments, and with names like Faraway, Royston and Ivanhoe. The builders have long since gone, but something of the same spirit remains, because the tea estates are run on very much the old lines, and the Indian Army has kept on the Staff College, with a large monument at the entrance declaring on its plinth, 'To die doing one's duty is glory.'

There are two clubs – the Wellington, with tennis courts and an eighteen-hole golf course, which is patronised mostly by the military, and the Coonoor club which has only tennis, used more by civilians. It does, however, have the best cream caramel, enlivened with nuts.

The golf has a quality quite of its own. There are about four level holes, while the rest climb or tumble down the steep hills, between the black-green trees of the forest and the bright emerald of the tea gardens. Two of the holes are so steep that players over sixty usually miss them as being too exhausting to get up. Cows and goats graze amiably on the fairways and traffic roars through the middle of several holes. Against that, it must be one of the most beautiful courses in the world and the cheapest.

My son, Nat, alarmed me by announcing that he had booked a course of lessons. In the event, the pro charged 30p for half an hour. Two young caddies, one of whom had a handicap of only four and was a good teacher, carried Nat's clubs and searched for his lost balls for a whole afternoon for the same sum.

There is one marked difference between the two clubs. At the Coonoor, as in every other civilian establishment in the State of Tamil Nadu, the beer comes with a warning on the label: 'Liquor; ruins country, family and life.'

In the Wellington, where the beer has a military provenance, there is no such gloomy warning. Is it that the army is thought impervious to evil, or that the State has no jurisdiction over the army, or simply part of the myth pattern of India?

Judging by the Colonel with whom I sat one morning it was certainly not the army's imperviousness to ruin. He had downed three vodkas by eleven o'clock. The State of Tamil Nadu has, of late, been more relaxed on the subject of alcohol, so I feel that the warning is one of those ambivalent areas of myth, so common in India. Drink is disapproved of, but nearly everybody drinks.

It was the Colonel's talk that reminded me of how little importance precision has in Indian life. He was telling me of a day with his men in the Himalayas. He needed to cross a pass at a height of 17,000 feet. Each man, including himself was carrying 72 kilos on his back.

If they failed to reach the top of the pass, a threatened demonic storm of thunder and lightning would shatter the rocks and fling the men into a chasm. If they failed to cross the pass that night, they would all die of cold. They must run. Run uphill, at that altitude, carrying the weight of another man?

'I made the fellows run and they jolly well did. We crossed the pass and not a man was lost.'

The military dominates the road from Coonoor to Ootacamund, with barracks and radio stations. The moment one arrives, one is conscious of a different spirit. Here is grandeur. The half-timbered villas are bigger. The classical porticos rise higher and the summit of it all is the Ooty Club.

The standards it maintains are hardly believable, good breeding, according to the secretary, being of paramount importance in any candidate for election. New money is unlikely to be elected and other attributes weigh heavily.

'Never marry a man who does not ride to hounds', the secretary advised a girl friend of mine, with no trace of humour.

The club itself which, not surprisingly, has a rather empty feeling is, in its way, a museum. The rooms are hung with trophies from the days when shooting tigers, elephants and any other creature that moved, was quite in order. Even today, the grandees of Ooty will don their pink coats and rush through the countryside in pursuit of a fox. Round the dining room are photographs of former MFHs.

The billiard room, in particular, has a Raj-nostalgic ambience. Round the huge table there are wicker-seated benches tilted back at an angle designed for lounging. On the walls are martial prints, many of them German (the result of a German secretary) others loyally British – Napoleon retreating from Moscow, a wild Highland charge, entitled, 'Scotland for ever'. It is strange to stand in this room with all its imperial associations, yet it is funny to think that it was here, in 1875, that another young subaltern called Neville Chamberlain, invented the game we see so much on television – snooker.

Something which evokes even more astonishment at the ways of the past is a visit to the loos. It is perhaps not odd that in the ladies there should be dressing tables and chairs for women to sit and chat while tidying up before dinner, but what sort of demand was there for armchairs and desks in the outer part of the gents? Was life so leisurely or so empty that while one's friend went to the lavatory one needed to sit down and write a letter?

The mists were rising and I remembered Burton. Even though there was a splendid house at Ooty called Crewe Hall, I was quite determined that I did not want to live in the Nilgiri Hills and we headed down the twisting road, bound for Kerala.

Some Catholic friends invited us to a disused synagogue to watch some Hindu dancing. In the lulls between the music, we could hear Muslims chanting verses from the Koran in the mosque next door.

Cochin, in Kerala, must be the most religiously tolerant place in the world. One pictures India as being torn apart by communal strife, but here people of every religion live in perfect amity.

Cochin has a long and jumbled history. It was a small sea-coast principality, ruled over by a Raja. Until the fourteenth century, most trade on this Malabar coast, known for its spices, was carried on through the more northern port of Kranganur. In 1341, the sea broke through the sand bank at Cochin that separated it from the long lagoon, known as the backwater, that runs inland, parallel with the sea, for a hundred miles or more. Thus Cochin became a natural, safe harbour.

As one goes through the streets of the old part of Cochin, the history of the place is revealed through the architecture. Nothing remains of the first arrivals, the Chinese, who settled on the left bank of the Calvethy river near its new mouth. When the Chinese left, driven out by the Arabs, the Hindus converted the building to their own use, throwing the statue of Buddha into the sea. The

Buddhist-cum-Hindu temple was finally destroyed by the Portuguese, who built on its site the original cathedral of Santa Cruz in 1515. A new one was built on the same site in 1902.

The cathedral was not the first church built by the Portuguese. Next to the large fort that they built in 1503, they put up at the same time a wooden church, replaced by a stone one forty years later, in which Vasco da Gama, the navigator, was buried. This church was appropriated by the Dutch, who kicked out the Portuguese in 1663, and taken over by the Anglican Church when the British seized power in 1795. It now belongs to the Church of South India.

Each group has left its mark in one way or another. At the water's edge rise peculiar triangular-shaped nets, suspended from a long pole, counterbalanced by a twenty-foot rope weighted with football-sized granite rocks, the whole thing working like a shadoof in Egypt. The nets are lowered into the water and raised again after fifteen minutes, with a great deal of heaving by four men, with remarkably few fish in them, at least whenever I am watching. These odd contraptions are said to be a legacy of the Chinese.

The Portuguese legacy would have been greater had it not been for the vandalism of the Dutch. On conquering the town, apart from killing and raping as many people as possible, they destroyed all but two of the twelve churches in the old town. They would have blown up the Vasco da Gama one, had the soldier ordered to do so not refused to destroy what he thought was a glorious piece of architecture. Worst of all, they burned to the ground what was

14

believed by scholars to be the finest library in the East.

By way of compensation perhaps, the most attractive buildings in old Cochin are the Dutch merchants' houses with their high tiled roofs, skilfully designed to take cooling advantage from the sea breezes.

The great British contribution was the result of one man's obsession. Robert Bristow was the chief engineer in the 1930s. He conceived the idea of making Cochin into the largest port in the Arabian Sea.

For five years he dredged, scooping out a channel deep enough to allow ships of 75,000 tons to come right into the harbour.

He incidentally dredged up the lost statue of Buddha. The Harbour Executive Officer, a Mr Milne, kept it in his office for a while and then took it back to England when he retired. Does it still sit in, say, Padstow or Grange-over-Sands, suitable material for an old-fashioned tale of a cursed idol?

With the silt, Bristow created a new island on which the docks were built and a railway terminal and today it also holds the airport.

Bristow was one of those happy people who achieve what everyone says is impossible. They all thought his island, made of sludge, would sink and that the bridge to it would collapse as soon as a train went over it. He loaded a long train with pig iron. In the middle was an ordinary coach. In this, he and his family sat. The train drove onto the bridge and there it sat while the Bristows confidently ate their picnic lunch.

Cochin is an irresistible place, blessed with an unusual harmony, relatively prosperous, pretty to look at and unspoilt by tourism and, therefore, free from beggars. It is odd to reflect that Kerala had, until last year, a freely elected Communist government. Everywhere the walls and even the roads are daubed with the hammer and sickle.

The docks, the source of much of the prosperity, have been idle for a week. A strike over some footling question of whether three boys who help to open the containers belong to the right union. Most people running an enterprise in Cochin try to employ people from the neighbouring state of Tamil Nadu. By doing that they are spared the labour problems created by the former Communist government.

Cochin might well be a delightful place to live, but I do not feel encouraged when I read in the local press that Communism is still the best way forward and that Stalin had all the right ideas, even if he had a few little failings on the humanitarian side.

After two weeks, I am still entranced by Cochin. It is the diversity of the people that is so intriguing. Its extraordinary cosmopolitan character was partly due to its successive conquerors.

But apart from the imperial nations, there were many religious groups from abroad, who have left a permanent mark on the place. The Arabs sent missionaries from the earliest times of Islam, and we are woken every morning at five by the Muezzin calling the faithful to prayer.

Then there were the Jews, who had built a synagogue not far away in 1344, just after the sand bar broke, opening the town directly to the sea. There is a theory that there had always been Jews in the area, the suggestion being that they had fled from the persecutions of Nebuchadnezzar in 587 BC. The present synagogue built in 1568 has, in one wall, a tablet taken from the 1344 building.

At some other period, a group of black Jews had also arrived. Their origins are obscure, although it is inevitably postulated that they were descendants of the Queen of Sheba. It was in their synagogue, abandoned because the last of them left for Israel in the 1950s, that, last week, we watched the Hindu dancing.

There are now only seven families of white Jews

remaining, comprising a community of twenty-five eld-
erly people. They, too, have nearly all gone to Israel.

I sat in the peaceful synagogue while a television crew
was filming an ancient survivor going through the rituals
of his prayer. A feeling of infinite sadness hung in this
beautiful place, with its brass pulpit, some rich Belgian
chandeliers and a magnificent floor of eighteenth-century
willow-pattern tiles brought from China.

The improbable legend has it that the tiles were intended as a gift from the Chinese Emperor to the Raja for
his new palace, but the Jews told him that cow's blood was
used in the making of the tiles, so he refused to use them
and gave them to the Jews, as thanks for their warning.

I asked if there were a Rabbi, hoping for more reliable
information, but was told that there had never been one.
Soon there will be no-one at all.

Hindus naturally predominate, being 60% of the population, but it is surprising to see even among them such
diversity, there being for instance, an enormous Jain temple. The Christians number 25%, among them some Syr-
ian Orthodox Christians, with a cheerfully gaudy church,
dedicated to both St Peter and St Paul.

Spiritual matters play a large part in everyone's life in
Cochin. The Catholic roomboy in our hotel begged me to
go to the place for which he was just leaving, to spend his
annual holiday in a retreat.

'Spend a week there and you will walk', he told me and
in a matter of days three other people urged to me to go
to this church, some fifty miles north.

If one takes a taxi, one can tell at once what religion the
driver is, for on the dashboard will be a plastic head of

Christ or a little Madonna and Child in the case of a Catholic, a simple cross for a Protestant, a picture of Parvati or Ganesh for a Hindu. Perhaps there are no Muslim taxi drivers, as I saw no Islamic symbol.

The Indians themselves can tell at a glance what religion anyone belongs to. Xavier, the young man I have taken to push my chair and act as interpreter, will point someone out in the street and say, 'He is a Gujerati.' How do you know? 'He wears those trousers, also you can see in his face.'

Even I have learned to tell a Muslim. All Keralan men wear a lunghi, the southern version of the northern dhoti. It is really just a piece of cloth, wrapped round the waist, reaching to the ankles. When out of doors they fold it in half, so that it reaches to just above the knees. It seems to me a most inconvenient garment as, at any given moment in the street, one man out of three is having to adjust his lunghi. Be that as it may, when they fold them up, Hindus and Christians tuck the ends in on the right, Muslims on the left.

There are also Muslim colours, especially green and some kinds of red, and large check patterns are more often used by them.

The gardener in our hotel looked to me like a regimental sergeant-major in a northern Maharajah's regiment. His lunghi was tucked in on the left. Is he really a Muslim, I asked Xavier? 'Oh no, he's a Hindu.' Then why does he fasten his lunghi on that side? 'Maybe he's left-handed, or maybe likes it better that side.' Rules are hard to establish.

As we roam through the town, Xavier explains that this

is a Catholic quarter and that a Muslim quarter, but in reality they all mix together, attending each other's festivals and celebrations. The big Christian festival is Carnival which happens at New Year. The main Hindu festival is Onam, a harvest festival in August or September. Absolutely everyone joins in both. The general community spirit is helped by everyone's speaking the same language – Malayalam. It does not sound too difficult to master and I have at least three words, but I am discouraged to hear from Xavier that there are fifty-six vowels.

This ecumenical spirit covers things other than religion. Medicine takes many forms – Western, Ayuvedic and Kerala's own medicine, Ayryavaidya, which involves massage with oils made from costly spices, and a number of other forms of medicine. Xavier has a small son of two, who has chest problems and frequently gets a high temperature, which brings on fits and convulsions.

He takes the child to a doctor ten miles away, at great expense. 'He is a Homeo doctor,' says Xavier, which I took to mean homeopathic, but now I am not sure. This week Kensal had another convulsion. Xavier took him to the doctor. When he came back, he said, 'It was our fault, we forgot and we bathed the boy on the day of the full moon and that was the cause of it.' I bought some paracetamol syrup for children. Will it work any better?

All day and sometimes all night, there was a ceaseless chinking sound that came over the wall of the court-yard of our hotel.

Curiosity made me knock on the high, sheet-iron gateway of the entrance to the place where the sound came from. The doorway opened a crack and a suspicious face peered out. Then came a big smile. 'You are a friend of Mr Prentice?' I mumbled a bit and the doorway swung wide.

On a half-acre space, leading down to the sea wall and a jetty, sixty-eight men were chipping away at blocks of granite, some of it white, some of it black. They worked under thatched shelters to protect them from the sun.

Pieces of sculpture stood in some places and, in others, what appeared to be a bordered pavement covered patches of the sandy ground. There was nothing Indian about any of the work.

The instigator of all this turned out to be an American sculptor of note, called Michael Prentice. He had been commissioned by the French to design a small square as a part of La Defense, the old quarter of Paris which was being entirely rebuilt in a spectacular flourish of architectural adventure.

At first, Michael Prentice had no particular plan in

mind, but on a visit to India, he happened to see a pile of granite that some shipper had got stuck with. He bought it for a fraction of what it would have cost in France.

Then, as he was driving along in Tamil Nadu, he saw some stone carvers working on a temple. He asked if they wanted some more work. In no time he had a full team of skilled stone workers, and from those happy chances he conceived his plans of four main pieces of sculpture set in an elaborately chiselled pavement.

Michael Prentice, a short man with a businesslike moustache, is one of those voluble, energetic men whose thoughts come out in a stream of even enthusiasm, rather like a ticker tape machine that reports the outbreak of war, the result of the 2.30 at Lingfield and a fall in the price of Glaxo with no change of emphasis. At one moment, he is discussing the French political situation, then he leaps to the cutlery and jewellery that he has been making at the same time as his sculptures for La Defense, then on to plans to build a hotel on the plot where he has been working, with a large rice boat, which would serve as a restaurant.

The work for France was finished this week. Michael looked at it and said, with his customary modesty, 'I don't know whether it's art, or what it is. But it doesn't matter, it's all fun.' With that, he flew off, the final stonework, the sixth container load was due to leave the next day. It was still there five days later. By then it was time for us to leave.

We bought a car. It is not like buying a car in Britain, and the negotiations took more than a week. We were promised delivery in three days, but in the same way that the stonework did not leave, the car did not arrive. Weary of the food in our hotel, we moved from Cochin to Quilon, a little more than fifty miles to the south. It is an uninteresting town, but our hotel is on the edge of the natural inland waterway that runs for a hundred miles or more, known as the backwater.

Marco Polo visited a town near here that he called Coilum. This is exactly how the locals pronounce Quilon, so I take it to be the same place. It was also here that Malcolm Muggeridge taught in a school on the backwater. He described it as paradise and in many ways it is.

We took a boat and have been wandering in and out of a positive maze of lakes and rivers and creeks and channels. All of life here is conducted on the water. Bright, multicoloured houses, yellows, blues, rich pinks, and purples, sit at the water's edge, surrounded by coconut palms.

Men fish, some from boats, some with those Chinese fishing nets we saw in Cochin. Women leave their washing and come down to the water to wave and laugh. They seem bolder here than in the towns. In front of some houses are piles of rice waiting to be loaded onto the high-prowed rice boats, with their look of a Venetian gondola. In front of others are coils of rope made from coconut fibre.

In small dugouts, children paddle themselves to school, scaring the cormorants that sit waiting on any stake projecting from the water. Noisy boats, with music blaring and decorated with tinsel and bunting, carry parties of pilgrims going to worship at the temple.

It is indeed a paradise and I toyed with the idea that this might be somewhere to live – quiet and hauntingly beautiful. The boatman tells me that I could buy a four-roomed house with its plot of coconut palms for £2,000. With my own motor boat I might live happily ever after. But I don't know. It is getting hot now. And soon the monsoon will come and rain and rain and rain for three months and I would be stuck in my little black and yellow house with its bright blue doors and the charm might fade.

As we drive along, I have developed a theory that the English learned to wash from the Indians. The stink of eighteenth-century Britain must have been appalling. Women often kept the same elaborate hairstyle for a month or more, crawling with nits, and people carried pomanders to ward off unpleasant smells. Washing was not high on anyone's list of priorities.

Driving through India, whenever one passes a patch of water, one can be sure that someone will be washing in it, either themselves or their clothes. It may just be coincidence but, in the nineteenth-century, as our contact with India became greater and more general, our cleanliness increased.

Car journeys can be long, often six or eight hours to go 250 miles, naturally including a couple of breakdowns and three punctures. Against that, they are never boring. The character of the country changes all the time and there is endless incident, pleasant or unpleasant. Yesterday, we stopped to fill a leaking radiator, a man in the house from which we got water was beating an eight-year old child who had played truant in the morning. The boy's mother tried to intervene, but the man was implacable and the child's screams rang in our ears for a long time.

There are bullocks working in the fields, looking as

they have looked for centuries; then suddenly there are thirty-two vast, modern, wind turbines, their propellers whirring like something in a science-fiction movie, generating electricity.

Even the longest drive is never dull, mostly beautiful, sometimes shocking and often humorous. Today, I saw a sign outside a small town advertising a bank from Madras as 'a shiny bank for a tiny district.' Nevertheless, as we go along, I am very conscious of missing a great deal through my ignorance.

Often there is a flag in a tree and I saw one on a rock in the middle of a pool. I gather that they mark places where a spirit resides, but I cannot be sure, especially in Kerala, where the Communists keep the red flag flying most assiduously.

Yesterday there was a stuffed figure of a man hanging from a palm tree. I sought an explanation for this from Xavier, who told me that it meant that someone was going to build a house on that site and that the doll was intended to tell other people not to be jealous. Soon after, we passed a temple where apparently a man was fasting for forty days and at the end of that time would have a hook put under the skin of his back, and as I understood it from Xavier's uncertain English, be somehow attached to a circular prayer wheel. For this he would be paid between ten and fifteen pounds and his employer be assured of his prayers bearing fruit.

This particular practice is nominally now illegal, but other even stranger ones, Xavier claims, still go on. We missed by a few days a festival at a temple at Cochin at which five men stand side by side and a long arrow is passed through their tongues, linking them together. Thus, inseparable, they dance. When the arrow is drawn out, they collapse, unconscious, to the ground. The priest dusts their tongues with a powder and half an hour later they are totally recovered, with no wound on their tongues.

We have moved now from the flat, lush green of southern Kerala with its pattern of waterways, into the drier state of Tamil Nadu with even a few bare, spiky mountains. We spent the night at Cape Comorin at the very southern tip of India. It is a holy place, because it was here that the goddess Parvati came to do penance in order to marry the god Shiva. Modern Hindus believe that they will be similarly cleansed if they bathe in the waters of the three seas which meet at this point.

Its holiness is somehow enhanced by the fact that you can watch the sun set, sinking into the Arabian sea and then in the morning, wake to see it burst out of the Bay of Bengal. Even more dramatic, at the time of the full moon, it is possible to see the moon rise at the same time as the sun sets.

Both the sunset and the sunrise this year glow a richer than ever red and gold with the dust from the Philippine volcano.

Alas, for all its holiness and interesting geographical situation, Cape Comorin is a tatty place, spoilt by the cheapest forms of touristic noise and trash.

The sunset and sunrise were indeed glorious, but we got almost as much pleasure from the menu in our hotel – an above average masterpiece of gobbledygook – Poride coats, scrampled eggs, chease, chicken Mary band, Guali flower.

We are now in temple land, moving, that is to say, from one great ancient city to another, the capitals of early South Indian dynasties – Madurai, Kanjipuram, Thanjavur, Tiruchirappalli, Mahabalipuram.

I think of the first time that I took my children to the circus. They watched the trapeze artists, the jugglers and the bareback riders, trying to look appreciative when I said, 'Isn't that amazing?'

When we got home, I asked what they had liked the most. 'Those seats we sat on that tip up when you get out of them.' The circus acts were, in a sense, no more surprising than so many other new things their young eyes saw every day. But the seats were something they could relate to.

I feel a little like that in these strange temples. Their gateways, covered with a myriad carvings of gods, dancers, weird figures and imaginary animals, rise to dizzy heights. Even today, when modern blocks surround them, they soar higher than any other buildings in the town.

We take off our shoes and roam through the huge complexes. Although the powerful dynasties have long since faded, these are still working temples, holy shrines used still by the devout Hindus. We go through the cloisters surrounding a pool. A large elephant stands outside one shrine. Its attendant orders it to bless me and it reaches out its trunk to touch my forehead. It has sharp hairs on the tip which prick my sunburn.

On the walls are frescoes. Below them sit groups of people, chatting. In dark corners, frail bundles of cloth turn out to be men sleeping. There are stalls selling temple cakes and in many places there is a stink of urine. A whole life goes on in these temples. Everywhere there are carvings – dancers with six arms, statues of Shiva or Krishna or Parvati in their many manifestations and disguises, with their confusing proliferation of names and aliases.

I can vaguely comprehend that it is all wonderful and in many cases beautiful, but I have never mastered the intricacies of the Hindu pantheon, nor read the tales of the Ramayana and the Mahabaratta, so that I am bewildered by the complexity of all the symbolism.

In the temple of Menakshi at Madurai, however, there is one thing that I found irresistible. On one wall there are two pillars each carved from one piece of stone. Some three feet up, the central pillar is surrounded by six slender columns, about two inches in diameter, all cut out of the same piece of stone. If you strike the central pillar with a pebble, it sounds exactly as you would expect. But if you tap the thin columns, each produces a different, pure musical note, so that you can play a tune on them. I could relate to that, but no-one could explain how it worked.

In a different way, the shore temples at Mahabalipuram are easily comprehensible, because they date from the seventh century, before Hindu art became so intricate. The temples stand a few yards from the sea and the winds of fourteen centuries have worn away much of the carving, but there is great charm in the simplicity of those works that have not been eroded. Courage, too, as most of the temples and the big statue of an elephant are carved out of the living rock.

Mahabalipuram must be the only place in the world where you can lie on the beach and pretend that you are having a cultural experience.

Secondhand car salesmen, as President Nixon might have said, are the same the world over. India is certainly no exception, so I will not weary you with the tale of the dud car I bought. The same thing could have happened in Tooting, San Francisco or Sydney.

Cars, on the other hand, are quite different in India. For years, there have really been only two kinds – the Ambassador and the Premier.

The Premier is a dull little thing, based originally on a small 1960s Fiat. The Ambassador is somehow rather splendid. It is a straight copy of a 1957 Morris Oxford.

For at least twenty years this was the car that served all purposes, from the grandest ministerial official car to the humblest rattletrap taxi.

There has been much in the theory that freedom is having no choice (think of the lack of fuss to be had from a set menu). Car bores and car snobs just did not exist in India. Of course, you could put on rows of spotlights or have fancy seat covers, but that was about the limit of showing off. The diesel version is the most popular because, while petrol costs roughly the same as in

England, diesel is one third of the price. 'I like it too', says my friend Mr Sen, 'because I can't hear my wife talking above the noise of the engine.'

A few years ago, this agreeable pattern was dented when the makers of the Ambassador introduced a flash thing called a Contessa, looking a bit like a small American Ford. It could even be fitted with air-conditioning. However, one does not see many of them about. They run only on petrol and cost £6,000, while a good wage for someone in middle management would be £3,000 a year.

Recently, there has been a flood of new possibilities, if you count four new choices as a flood. The most popular new thing is a minibus called an Omni made by Maruti, though it is really a Suzuki. It is an 800 cc. affair with only three cylinders, yet it is surprisingly nippy, being very low geared. Its top speed is little over 50 m.p.h. but, Indian driving being what it is, that is quite enough. Then there is a Mahindra Jeep, which is just a diesel van, a four-wheel drive Maruti Gypsy and, newest of all, a Sierra, made by Tata, that costs an unimaginable £10,000. I find this rush of modernity all rather sad, as I wait for my tottering Ambassador to be repaired.

South India is obsessed by films. Even quite small towns have large art-deco cinemas, well worthy of being called picture palaces. Half of India's cinemas are in the four main southern states. The town of Bangalore, according to Louise Nicholson's excellent guide book has 150 cinemas, forty of them in the same street. In Tamil Nadu, the last Chief Minister was an actor and the new one is an actress.

I was sitting in the hallway of our hotel. From outside there came a sudden hooting and shouting. A car drew up. At once, a surging mob of young men and boys surrounded it, yelling and pushing. Kamala Hassan, a film star, had arrived. The crowd shouted and screamed, far louder and hoarser than a horde of teeny boppers in pursuit of a pop idol, which made them seem rather menacing.

The star managed at last to get out of his car and into the lobby. The security guards did not even bother to try to keep the crowd out. They surged into this rather posh hotel, yelling and shoving. They were not exactly rough, but they were a mob of excited youths. It was not quite clear what they wanted, but primarily I think it was to touch him, as many of them nearest to him started pushing out again.

The star had only come to change in the hotel before giving a lecture in town, in aid of some charity. While he was upstairs, the crowd of three or four hundred, with not one woman or girl among them, waited outside. Our room had a balcony and when my son Nat went out on it to look at the crowd, they all cheered and yelled. Slightly envious, I went out and gave a few Queen Motherly waves and was gratified to get an equal share of the cheering.

One thing has been puzzling me. In every town and village there are masses of goats, mostly foraging on the rubbish heaps. Plainly many of them are kept for their milk, as I see that many of the nanny goats have bags over their udders to prevent the kids from drinking all their milk.

I never see goat on the menu in even the cheapest restaurants. I asked Xavier, my helper, about this wondering whether there was some religious prohibition about eating goat meat, although Muslims and Jews happily eat it. Of course, strict Hindus eat no meat of any kind.

'Oh no,' said Xavier, 'we eat a lot of goat. Haven't you seen mutton on the menu? You see, mutton is goat.' I was glad to have that cleared up and, come to think of it, I have not seen one sheep.

There are fifteen official languages in India. English is called an associate language. Most officials speak it fairly well and the better educated classes use it very often as their first language, because the jumble of Indian languages and dialects (said to number 1,652) makes it impossible for Indians, particularly in the south, to speak to anyone outside their own state.

What fascinates me is the kind of English they speak.

Very often it is almost absurdly correct or preposterously out of date, with cries of 'Jolly good show' or 'That's ripping.' But I find more intriguing the words that I cannot understand or have never heard used. 'I have been to England thrice,' someone said to me last week and this morning, when I asked how far it was to the bookshop, the hotel manager said, 'It is just over two furlongs.'

Many of the obscure words are associated with motor cars. The boot is known as the dickey. To me a dickey is what the Americans call the rumble seat, which is to say a thing at the back which, indeed, opened rather like a boot, but downwards to reveal an open-air seat. But what is a stepney? The answer is a spare wheel. This seemed so bizarre that I did a bit of research.

Evidently, in the early days of pneumatic tyres, before anyone thought of carrying a spare, there was a round wooden thing, slightly bigger than the wheel, that you clamped on to the side of the wheel and limped to a garage to have your puncture mended. You might think that they were made in Stepney. No. Apparently they were made in Wales by a company called Stepney.

This confusion of Indian languages has meant a change in our lives. Xavier, who has been pushing my wheelchair, comes from Cochin in Kerala, where they speak Malayalam. Going through Tamil Nadu, where they speak Tamil, he has managed well enough. The two languages are fairly similar. Now we are going into Andhra Pradesh, where they speak Telugu. Although this is also a Dravidian language, he says he cannot manage it, so he is going home to his wife and child in Cochin.

I have taken on a 22-year old driver from Mahabalipuram, called Selvum. He was working as a taxi driver and earned £2.50 a week. This was an improvement on his previous job as a motorcycle mechanic, which brought in £1.50 a week. He was now able to save £1 a week, with a view to one day opening his own motorbike repair shop.

I offered him £4 a week to drive my shambling car. He consulted his father, who told him to take the job. Selvum's father works, by feudal arrangement, one acre of indifferent sandy land on which he grows rice. He divides the takings from the sale of the crop fifty-fifty with the landowner. That, apart from what Selvum earns, is the total income of his family of a wife and six children. Selvum's older brother had a good education and hopes for a job in government service, but it needs a bribe of £400 to be sure of getting one. His three other brothers are younger than he is. One of his two sisters is getting married next month. The dowry that his father must pay is £500.

Xavier tells me that that is cheap. In Cochin, it is quite normal to pay £2,000. How do people do it?

'They borrow,' says Xavier, 'an Indian is born in debt, lives in debt and dies in debt.'

Madras is one of those cities, like Lima in Peru, that everyone says must have been wonderful in the old days. Even Kipling, in whose time it was surely magnificent, compared Madras to a 'withered beldame brooding on ancient fame.' He was writing within only a few years of the building of the most grandiose structures of the British empire.

In eighteenth century Madras, the British put up recognisably Georgian pieces of architecture, many of them very pretty. The nineteenth century saw the invention of an extraordinary style known as Indo-Saracenic. Vast, wild red buildings with towers and cupolas, porticos and parapets, pillared halls and vaulted cloisters, doorways tall enough for giants, great sweeps of stairways. The architects drew on the traditions of the Moghuls, the designs of the Moors, the patterns of the Venetians and the proportions of Palladio to produce a fantastical form of splendour that should be absurd, but is successfully impressive.

Sadly, the withered beldame's clothes now hang in tatters. In the general chaos of the city that has grown up in its own way since Independence, some of the splendours remain, but usually only those with a public use. Much has been torn down and even more is threatened.

There is nothing vengeful about this. There are still statues to Queen Victoria and other British royalty, but unless a building is used by the Government, or becomes an institute, a college, a club, or an hotel, as in the case of the Connemara where I am staying, it is probably doomed.

Occasionally, amid the spread of skyscrapers, modern villas, small factories and slums, one spots a little gem of a Regency house with tottering pillars and rusting iron balconies. It is abandoned and crumbling. Next year it will be gone.

Some grand Indo-Saracenic marvels remain – the Law Courts, said to be the largest in the world after London, the Central Station and next to it the incredible grey-granite palace of the Southern Railway's offices, looking as if it should be in Mysore as one of the Maharaja's huge mansions or in Whitehall as a gigantic ministry. Others are desolate – a tree grows out of the fanciful cupola of one of the remaining wings of Spencer's famous depart-ment store on the main shopping street, Mount Road.

Yet there are unlooked for delights. The Icehouse still stands near the beach where, until the 1870s, the improbably-named Tudor Ice company stored the ice that it imported from New England.

In the middle of Mount Road, I puzzled over Sir Francis Chantrey's equestrian statue of the 1820s Governor, Sir Thomas Munro. He is dressed in fine clothes, but his legs dangle oddly, as he has no stirrups, indeed no saddle.

Talking of Governors, my hotel, most people suppose, was called after an 1890s' governor, Lord Connemara. In fact, it was called after his wife. The house was originally built by an English surgeon called Binny, who became the adviser to the Nawab of Wallagah, Prince of Arcot. He bought the Nawab's garden house in 1815 and did it up in style. It was sold when Binny died, and became an hotel.

Lord Connemara was a friend of the Nawab's descendant. This later Nawab used to satisfy the Governor's unfortunate tastes by supplying him with very young girls.

Lady Connemara got to hear of this and she fled from Government House to what was then, and still is, the city's most elegant hotel. At that time, it was called the Imperial, but was later renamed the Connemara in her honour. She never left it until the Governor retired and they went home to Britain.

In the last fifteen years, the changes in Madras have not been purely physical. In fact, my friends Mr Gopan and Mr Shivaraman, with whom I sat one afternoon, told me that there is now a move to try to preserve the old buildings. The major change has been a social one.

Until quite recently Madras was an extremely conventional place, regarded by Delhi and Calcutta as rather provincial in its primness. There was never such a thing as a disco and the proprieties between the sexes were most scrupulously observed.

My friends say that this has now all changed. Boys and girls go out together and form love matches. Madras has several discos, playing imitation pop music, based on American and British music, with an Indian twang and the most bizzare words. The refrain of one of them goes, 'It's a beautiful world, it's a jolly good world. You are sixteen, I am seventeen, let's go and make marry.' The fact that marriage is suggested might make one think that restraint is still important to the young, but slipped in, are some fairly suggestive lines.

I have seen people kissing in the street, which would have been unthinkable ten years ago. The Indian cinema was, for a long time, known for the superficial chastity of the relations between the sexes. The posters advertising the films are lurid and provocative, but the content, on the whole, is still not sexually adventurous.

The worries of Madras parents seem to be taking on a pattern familiar in Europe. Drugs are a considerable anxiety, as they are all over India. In Cochin, I was told of an exceptionally good, expensive private school, where numbers of the girls resorted to prostitution to pay for their habit. There was, inevitably in India, where myth springs eternal, the story of a rich businessman going to a hotel and sending out for a girl for the night, only to be presented with his own daughter.

The changes are not only in the habits of the young. Divorce was, until recently, extremely rare, and a divorced woman had no hope of another marriage. 'Now', said Mr Gopan, 'it is nearly a positive advantage.'

The one thing that never seems to change is the question of a dowry. Mr Shivaraman has three daughters. I asked him if this was not going to be very expensive for him. To get them each a husband, he would have to pay out at least £2,000 apiece.

'Really, I do not mind. The money will be no use to me when I am dead and I will die happy to think that each of them has a well-to-do husband. By well-to-do, I mean well-educated. Anyone can lose his money, but no one can take away a good education.'

The new freedoms of Madras were, I imagined, attributable to videos which, to judge by the films available in the better hotels, are pretty vivid and explicit.

'No, videos are quite out of date,' said Mr Gopan, 'the big influence is Star TV. Everybody has it and they can learn anything from that.'

Star TV is a satellite network. It works on the same lines as Sky TV and is beamed out of Hong Kong all over the East and Australia, broadcasting films, sport, much trash and the excellent BBC World Service which, in India at any rate, appears to have replaced CNN in the viewers' affections.

I don't know whether the man who reeled up to the table next to ours, in what is luckily an outdoor restaurant in the Connemara, was a product of the new order, or simply an example of different manners. He threw up all over the ground next to his table – the most voluminous vomit I have ever witnessed. His companions were not much put out, but greeted his performance with cries of, 'Oh my goodness, fountain plaza, fountain plaza.' The man went happily on with his dinner and the hotel staff, as one might expect from such an establishment, paid no attention, but went courteously about the business of mopping up the mess.

It struck me as we left Madras what a green city it must look from the air. Everywhere there are gardens and, even in the dingiest quarters, there is a profusion of trees, most of them, at the moment, in glorious flower – the Rain trees forming green umbrellas spotted with pink, the Cassias a spread of butter yellow and the first of the Flamboyants a rich leafless red.

It was an impression I soon forgot as we drove north through the state of Andhra Pradesh. Here the land is dry and inhospitable. There are a few bare hills, but mostly it is dreary and flat, apart from sudden piles of enormous boulders, deposited by heaven knows what volcanic upheaval. Beside the boulders are factories, where workers chip endlessly at the stones, day and night, to satisfy Indians' evidently insatiable need for what I believe in road-builder's terms is called 'chatter.'

There was little to relieve the tedium of fourteen-hour car journeys except for the countless little incidents that make India so beguiling.

A puncture. And, as I wait, a drunk pesters me to accept some coconut water as a gift. I give in and he brings it, spilling most of it over me and then wants 20p for it. He turns out to be a bank manager – 'a drinking bank manager, you understand,' he says with an engaging smile.

There are always overturned lorries and buses and hideously crushed cars to spark ghoulish speculation, though it is tinged with wondering whether it will be our turn next. We came to a bridge with a sinister warning – 'Weak bridge. Go slow. Only one vehicle to cross at one time.' I noticed the number plate of the car in front of us: TAY 1879. 1879? Was that not the year of the Tay Bridge disaster? I kept telling myself, as we crossed, that I am not superstitious. But I was quite relieved when we reached the other side in safety.

More agreeably, in every village one goes through, there are pretty girls to look at, shy, with flirting eyes. They dress in brilliant colours so that they stand out from the grey-brown surroundings, their hair woven with flowers down their backs.

Surprises are endless, blunting ennui. We stopped for lunch at a wayside café. Another car drew up behind ours. On its roof was a tangled mat half-an-inch thick, looking a little like shredded wheat. Even though we were several yards away from the car, a delicious smell wafted towards us. The mat was made of Vetiver, the aromatic root of an Indian plant. The owner of the car was exceedingly proud of this curious mat.

'I would like you to know, sir, that Vetiver has this most useful property. It keeps everything around it cool. While you are very, very hot in your car on this scorching day, I in my car am as cool as cucumbers. It is as good as air-conditioning, but it cost me only 600 rupees, instead of many thousands.'

There is also the surprise that many people ask if we are Russian. This east coast of India seems to be very popular with Russians, to the extent that in one hotel there were notices in Cyrillic script.

The culminating horror of Andhra Pradhesh came at the seaside resort of Vishnakapatnam. Nat's birthday started badly. Our ugly hotel of ill-contrived modernity sat eighty yards back from what appeared to be an attractive beach. In the event, it was dirty and the currents dangerous. When Nat went down to swim in the morning, he found a dead man lying at the water's edge. He had plainly drowned and his head had been bashed on the rocks. He cannot have been long dead because, as the waves nudged him against the sand, his limbs sprawled and twisted, moving freely with each new buffet of the sea. In the end, one larger wave brought the man up onto the dry sand, somehow managing to leave him flat on his back, his arms folded neatly across his chest, his eyes thinly closed.

Nat tried to interest some other people on the beach in the poor man's fate. They told him to leave everything alone and to go back to the hotel. 'Don't get involved, it will only cause you trouble.'

At the hotel, the manager virtually forbade him to speak to the police. 'It is better to forget all about it. If the police come and you were the first to find the body they will ask all of us awkward questions. They will want to know everything and they will keep you here for days, even weeks, until they are satisfied.'

Nat protested that it was quite obvious what had happened, as the dead man was wearing swimming-trunks. He had gone for an early morning swim and either got swept onto the rocks and then drowned or the other way round. Nat was worried about the man's family, who would presumably soon be anxious to know what had become of him.

Any Indian to whom one mentions this story says that they were all giving sound advice. Never get involved with the police.

One of the surprises of India, for all the diversity of its culture, its glorious architecture, its ancient literature, its sophisticated cinema, its industrial development and the density of its population, is the wildness of some areas. And even more surprising in these areas is the simplicity of the people, known as tribals, whose way of life and customs bear little or no relation to the mainstream of Indian life.

The State of Orissa, on the east coast, south of Calcutta, is one of Indian's poorest regions and about a quarter of its population are tribals. In the hilly interior of the State live a mixture of some sixty-two tribes, each one speaking a different dialect. From a tourist's point of view, the most famous are probably the Bondas, the naked people, known for their free and easy sexual habits.

I have a priggish aversion to going to gaze at people as one might look at animals in a zoo, so we did not go to see the Bondas, but came instead to an area inhabited by the Bhyan and a few Munda, where a friend of mine, Basant Dube, has started a tea plantation, the only one in Orissa. It is a somewhat rash undertaking as the climate is not as humid as it should be; the volcanic soil, rich in iron, is not ideal and, because of indiscriminate tree-felling, there is little topsoil; and the nearest town, where only the most basic things are available, is a bumpy hour-and-a-half away.

Nonetheless, it is an enchanting place. The tea bushes, 14,000 of them to a hectare, sit tightly-packed and trimmed to thigh level, so flat that they look like a tufted carpet, laid under some 500 Albizzia shade trees. On our first morning, we were out early to see the plucking of the tea leaves. It was a sight of poignant beauty. More than a hundred girls moved quietly through the clustered bushes. Their brilliant saris – reds, sharp blues, saffrons and yellows – stood out from the uniform green of the tea and shone bright in the speckled shafts of sunlight.

The people of the Bhuyan tribe are small with distinctive features, their noses recessed at the top between their deep-set eyes. It was easy to pick out the few Mundas, taller and with broader faces. The girls were sweetly shy, but friendly. The manager warned us not to be too familiar with them, in case their menfolk took it amiss.

Not long ago, the tribals of Orissa were all, and in some cases still are, hunter-gatherers. Gradually most of them have taken to some form of agriculture, at first a shifting cultivation, planting for one season, burning the land after the harvest and moving on.

The Bhuyan, because they are now confined to a narrower area, have passed on to another stage, known to experts as podo-culture. This means alternating between two places. Despite these concessions to modernity, the tribals hanker after their old customs. They still hunt with bows and arrows, arrows tipped with razor-keen heads or fearsome three-pronged affairs, 'good for wounding in the stomach' and might not be above shooting anyone who made advances to their women.

More alarming are the sloth bears that roam through the gardens in the evenings and the early mornings. They belie their name, being swift and ferocious. Attacking quite gratuitously, they rise on their back legs, standing five feet tall, smashing down their clawed front paws onto their victims, choosing always the face of a person to savage. Nearly every week someone in the region is mauled. The nightwatchman showed me the terrible scars on his head, the result of an encounter with a bear.

My friend, Mr Dube, when I told him of my search for somewhere to live in India, offered me ten hectares of land here to farm in any way that I wanted – coffee, cashew nuts, orchids, or even more tea. I was entranced by this wild, lost place, with its sudden rivers, rocky hills and its proud people. But I do not think I any longer have the energy to live in quite so remote a spot.

We went to the coast and to the holy places of Orissa. As usual, the way was full of event. In one village, a crowd of men was rushing and shouting. Apparently, a saddhu or holy man had kidnapped a young boy, quite why was unclear, but the mob was out to avenge the crime. Luckily for the holy man, he had already been caught by the police and was fairly safe in the local jail.

In Cuttack, there was another uproar. Two hundred or more people had died from drinking hooch, and many more were blinded. Everyone knew the man who was responsible, a man who had made a fortune from illicit liquor, but he had powerful connections and was unlikely to be arrested.

Agriculture being still uppermost in my mind, I was distressed to see, as we neared the coast, thick masses of water hyacinth in full, delicate mauve flower. It was everywhere, in the rice fields, in the irrigation canals and in every pool. This plant of treacherous prettiness has come from Africa, where it has clogged rivers and waterways and, seemingly impossible to control, now threatens to engulf many of India's waters in the same way.

At Konarak, we stopped to look at the largely ruined but still astonishing thirteenth-century temple, built of stone and shaped like an immense chariot, with twenty-four huge wheels, each of which alone is twice the height of a man. The temple is covered all over with thousands of carvings, many of them erotic, from tiny ones on the spokes of the chariot wheels to larger than life-sized ones inside the temple.

The town of Puri, a little further down the coast, is also associated with chariots. The temple here is dedicated to the Hindu god, Lord Jagganath. Every year the people of Puri make vast chariots of wood, so big that it takes 4,000 men to pull them, in order to take the gods out for a week's holiday near the beach. It is from Lord Jagganath that we get the word juggernaut for our large lorries.

Because Puri is such a holy city, though the connection may not be immediately obvious to everyone, it is perfectly legal to buy cannabis and opium there. In fact, there are authorised government shops selling the stuff.

The shops are sad places, with wooden grilles, behind which lurk unsympathetic salesmen, catering to pathetic queues of addicts, who proffer the equivalent of 6p for a minute lump of opium. The sophisticated rickshaw driver advised us against buying the government 'grass'. It was rough stuff that would make one cough. The black market, he said, would provide far better 'grass', brought from Kerala. The opium, too, he said, was adulterated with black rice and might make one sick. Again, the black market could provide for less than a pound excellent opium, soft and pliant and capable of inducing delightful dreams. Here it would appear that opium is the religion of the people.

I have been to Calcutta many times, but I always feel a little ashamed when I say how much I like the place. How can one like a city where the people are so poor that hundreds sleep in the streets; where the hovels that the more fortunate have are so wretched one would not offer them to a goat; where the pollution is so grim that one has to change one's shirt three times a day?

The answer to these awkward questions lies in the spirit of the people and in the cultural tradition of the city.

Life is, in so many ways, so awful that the only way to survive is to try to enjoy it. The people, peering from their hovels or washing in the gutter as one passes, will laugh and joke as if there were nothing to worry about. They love my electric wheelchair. If I stop in the street, I will soon have a crowd around me begging to know how it works and, inevitably, how much it costs. And, as I go, I gather a following of anything up to fifty ragged, inquisitive children, jostling and chattering, so that I feel like the Pied Piper.

Calcutta, far more than Bombay or Delhi, is the cultural centre of India. It is here that the good Indian films are produced, as opposed to the glittery nonsense that comes out of Bombay and it is the home of Indian literature. Apart from the Indian Museum, which is possibly the best museum in the country, there are at least a dozen other museums. The Botanical Gardens, where the plants for the development of the tea industry in Darjeeling and Assam were cultivated in the last century, is a peaceful and singular pleasure.

On the birthday of Rabindranath Tagore, the philosopher and poet, who won the Nobel Prize for literature in 1913, I went to the Spastics Centre, a modern building put up by a charity, to watch a performance of a play by Tagore, celebrating the beginning of Spring. It was put on by the spastic and handicapped children, who are cared for by the centre. It was beautifully done, both happy and very moving. I am doubtful whether anything so encouraging and worthwhile could take place in any other Indian city.

The pollution and grime is too great a problem for anyone to do anything about. It was recently highlighted in an unusual way. Jane McAusland, the distinguished English restorer of art on paper, was working in the Victoria Memorial. This grandiose, white marble building, a last flourish of Empire, finished in 1921 and looking like a vast Castle Howard with Moghul touches, houses some marvellous examples of British painting, including the works of water colourists William Daniell and his nephew, Thomas.

Jane has an interesting way of treating prints which, as she admits, sounds rather alarming. She puts them out in baths of water, under transparent sheets of polyester and bleaches them in the sun to remove foxing and staining. Of course, she only leaves them out briefly so there is no danger of fading the prints or harming the paper.

She tried this out in Calcutta. On the first day, she was puzzled that it did not work. She tried again the next day with great success, the spots and marks disappeared as they should. It happened that on that day there was a transport strike – all the buses and taxis were off the streets. The air, for once, was comparatively clear and the sun could do its work.

Because Calcutta was the capital of British India for all but the last thirty-six years, the imprint of the Raj is stronger here than in any other city. In contrast to Madras, where the architecture in the last century took on a wild, exotic combination of Victorian gothic and Moghul fantasy, the buildings of Calcutta were sedately classical. Had the climate not inflicted almost immediate decay, the city might have an air similar to Nash's London.

The buildings now crumble, but there are other strange legacies in out of the way corners. In a small back street there is a shop, which one well might pass without a second glance. It has a green doorway, half closed, either side of which is the hammer and sickle symbol of the Marxists who govern the city.

Here, Mr Manik Lal Das follows the silversmith's trade. I had been told by a romantic, that his little business, which goes under the name Kalipada Das, was entitled to put a hallmark on his work and that that mark was recognised in London.

Mr Das, a jovial, grey-haired man with cheeks that puff out when he smiles, laughed at this idea and had to admit that it was quite untrue. Nonetheless, his family have carried on this business for four generations, their customers being mostly British. He does stamp his silver with the letters KPD, his father's initials, but he did not know what mark his family had used before that, nor could he remember his grandfather's name.

The workmanship coming out of this tiny establishment is superb. Mr Das showed me tributes from Ambassadors, High Commissioners and all manner of dignitaries praising both his and his late father's craftsmanship. Mr Das can reproduce almost anything, even from a photograph, making it, according to one High Commissioner, indistinguishable from the original.

Even today, he can make, say, a spoon or a fork, looking as if it had been made by Paul Lamerie for as little as ten pounds. A whole Georgian service for eight place settings could cost under six hundred pounds.

It tickled me to think of those grand Memsahibs summoning Mr Das or his ancestors and commissioning them to make some pieces of fine silver. They would never have known or believed the hole in the wall where their copies of a Georgian candlestick had actually been made. And I hope there are still on British dining tables pieces of the Das family's work, masquerading as priceless Georgian silver.

Sadly, Mr Das's trade had dropped off. There are no more Memsahibs and his principal work now seems to be making trophies and cups for sporting events or an occasional civic emblem. Nor will there be another generation to carry on the family tradition. Mr Das has two sons, but he says he does not want them to go into the business. 'The difficulties are too many. There is the labour problem, there is the interference and there are not the customers.'

I did not like to ask him whether the symbols at his door might not have something to do with it.

His address is: Manik Lal Das, 21A Sambhunath Pandit Street, Bhowanipur, Calcutta 700025.

Although the government of West Bengal is Marxist, there are, at any rate in Calcutta, the capital of the state, many things that seem incompatible with orthodox communism. There is the best racecourse in India; there are the showy weddings of the rich Marwari families, to which the women guests come shimmering with diamonds and emeralds, while the crowds gaze in uncomplaining wonder at such unabashed displays of wealth; above all, there are the clubs, relics of the days of the British Raj, still havens of privilege even in modern India.

The most unexpected of these is the Tollygunge Club, an oasis of peace and greenery in the grime and clamour of this astonishing city. The early nineteenth-century clubhouse, once a private house, sits in 100 acres of parkland dotted with flowering trees.

There is an 18-hole golf course, cunningly woven into the rather small area, not quite the rival of the Calcutta Golf Club (the oldest course in the former British Empire), but an agreeable place to play, with beautifully kept greens. There are grass and clay tennis courts, squash courts, an indoor and an outdoor swimming pool, stables with horses to ride and all manner of other diversions as well as two restaurants and bars.

The membership mostly consists of the businessmen of

Calcutta, who bring their wives and families at the week-ends. It is popular, too, with the many foreign diplomats, whose countries have consular or commercial representation in the city. It may be partly on account of these diplomats that the West Bengal government is so tolerant of this spacious island of luxury in an area that might otherwise be ripe for development. With no Tollygunge for their staff to escape to, some diplomatic missions might well close down.

But it is not just foreign officials who find refuge there. I woke one morning at six and, looking out of my window (there are also rooms to let to non-members), I was surprised to see soldiers in black uniforms, armed with automatic weapons, lurking behind several bushes. It turned out that they were the bodyguard of General Brar, the Commander-in-Chief of Eastern Command, who had come for an early round of golf.

General Brar is the Sikh officer whom Mrs Gandhi ordered to invade the sacred Golden Temple at Amritsar, asking him whether he was first a soldier or a Sikh. The unfortunate general is under threat not only from the usual run of terrorists – the Tamil Tigers, the Assamese separatists, the Kashmiri militants, the Naxalites, but also from some of his own people – Sikh extremists who regard him as a traitor. Hence the 'black cats' as his protectors are called.

The Tollygunge Club must be one of the pleasantest country clubs in the world and much of its excellence is attributable to the man who runs it, an Englishman of unsurpassed geniality, Bob Wright.

Bob, a handsome man of sixty-seven, with a faintly

military bearing, was born in India. But he left as a child and did not return until after the war, when he worked in Calcutta for a company with diverse interests, ranging from coal and oil to tea. His wife, Anne, was brought up in India, the daughter of a senior official in the British Indian Civil Service.

How Bob came to run the Tollygunge is an odd story. Some twenty years ago, the Naxalite troubles in Calcutta were at their height. There were many acts of terrorism and much stirring up of labour unions.

A couple of the staff at the Club had been dismissed for stealing. In revenge, the terrorists invaded the Club and shot dead the Secretary in his office.

Shocked and frightened, the members panicked. They called a meeting at which most of them were strongly in favour of closing the Club and selling the land. Bob was, by this time, the member of longest standing. He protested firmly that they should not give in to terrorism. He offered to take over the Secretary's duties, just temporarily, to sort out the labour problems and to keep things running. Two decades later, he is still there.

He and Anne used to have a fine house, with a fair bit of land, on which they bred horses. Unfortunately, in rather distressing circumstances, they lost their house. Having nowhere to live, it seemed sensible to move, at any rate temporarily, to the flat at the top of the club building. As usual with the Wrights' temporary arrangements, it has gone on for fifteen years and they preside over this delightful club, loved by everybody.

It is odd to think that he took over the running of the club partly because the staff were unhappy. This year, when he was going away to England, the staff threw a farewell party for him. There were speeches, begging him to hurry back; there were even tears in some people's eyes. One would have thought that he was going away for years, possibly forever. He was, as everyone knew, merely going for a three-week break.

Altogether Bob is an extraordinary man. There is no end to the committees he sits on and the good works that he is involved in. Whenever anything is in danger of folding up in Calcutta, the organisers come to him and ask him to save whatever it is – an historic graveyard, a conservation scheme, a charity for the homeless. With his soft heart, he agrees and soon pumps life into the fading enterprise.

All this leaves him little time for himself, yet he and his wife have created in the Kanha National Park, in distant Madhya Pradesh, a safari camp to which they can escape in the winter months. There, their daughter Belinda, a talented maker of TV documentaries, is much involved in a project for the protection of tigers, with such success that the tiger population of the park has more than doubled in recent years.

Bob has done much for Calcutta and for India as a whole. One cannot help feeling that, if only the British in India had been more like him, with his understanding of and his affection for the people he lives among, the Empire might have had a happier ending.

While I was in Calcutta, I had a letter from Humphry Berkeley, asking me to contribute to a collection of essays entitled *Was it a Miracle?* He is going to make a book of these to raise money for leukaemia. I thought that

Mother Teresa should know about miracles. I went to visit her in her convent. I asked if she would like to write one of the essays. She refused, 'I never do anything for fund-raising, the Lord will provide.' She is certainly an austere person. She looked at me and said, 'You have a disability. It was a gift from God, use it.' I was startled by this, but when I pondered on it for some time, I came to the conclusion that she was right.

In Hindi, the word for yesterday and the word for tomorrow are the same. They are both Kal. The difference is achieved by the context, the tense used, or just by an accompanying twist of the hand, a clockwise swivel meaning tomorrow, an anti-clockwise one indicating yesterday.

India does not become clearer as time goes on; it becomes hazier and more confusing. Things that we in the West assume are opposites here blend together into forms we find it hard to encompass. Truth mingles easily with fantasy, evil can have some attributes of good, most noticeably tenderness and violence go hand in hand.

I have been reading Gillian Tindall's latest excellent novel, *Spirit Weddings*. It is set mostly in an imaginary far eastern country, possibly an amalgam of India, Thailand and Malaysia, with touches of Singapore, Hong Kong and Calcutta thrown in. The book captures exactly the underlying sense of unease that pervades India and so much of the East.

How can all these gentle smiling people have a side to them of such extreme violence? Think of the sweet Cambodian whose Hyde-side is a Khmer Rouge executioner; the beaming Jekyll of a boy in Sri Lanka, who is a Tamil Tiger torturer; the bowing Japanese, who can be so readily incited to Samurai excesses.

So much of everyday life in India is tinged with menace. Each day's newspaper has tales of death and murder and kidnapping. At random, from the last couple of days:

Forty injured and one man dead – a naked wire falling from a tube-light had touched a railing against which worshippers were leaning at a temple.

Fifteen dead from an explosion at a Bombay hotel.

A young wife set herself and her baby on fire. Her husband is accused of complicity in the tragedy. His family had been pestering her about the unpaid dowry.

(In Kerala 30% of young wives commit suicide. Their husbands are usually away working in the Middle East, and the girls' in-laws torment them.)

One killed and eleven injured in a fracas, because a shopkeeper refused to repair the transistor belonging to someone of a different caste.

Three children found dead in Delhi's drains. Two are believed to have been murdered; the third, a toddler of two, may have fallen off a train.

These events, of course, take no account of such disasters as a lorry crashing into a tree, twenty of the labourers riding in the back being killed and fifty injured.

Talking of East-West contrasts, I am reminded of a preposterous article that appeared in Queen magazine at the time when Japan entered the Second World War. Jennifer, or her equivalent, believed that British fighter pilots would have the edge over any aviators the Japanese might put up, because the British officers would have such 'good hands', as a result of their experience in the hunting field.

Today, I am struck by the extraordinary ineptitude of the Indians in practical, physical matters. When it comes to helping me in my wheelchair, it is not that they are not willing to help. In that way they are far more forthcoming than English people. They rush, with eager offers of assistance, but they always get into a muddle. Getting me into a car, they will stand on the wrong side, so that they are in the way. They are seemingly determined to carry me upside down and so on.

This inability is not limited to dealing with me. Faced with loading luggage into a car boot, they can get in only about half of what my son, Nat, packs in.

I have been seeking an explanation for this. It is not a question of intelligence. The feats of mental arithmetic that many a child of six in the bazaar can perform would put most British fifteen-year-olds to shame. It must be a result of conditioning. Is it too Jennifer-like to wonder whether it is a failure of co-ordination, attributable to a lack of physical games in childhood?

The average Indian child has no toys, no chance of playing any game, nothing that might give him the experience of working out so much that is automatic to a British child.

A friend suggests another explanation. Throughout the centuries the rich have discouraged the poor from thinking for themselves. If you have one thought, it may well lead you on to another and the last thing top dogs want is for underdogs to start using their imagination and having revolutionary thoughts. Getting young Indians to work things out for themselves means breaking down generations of conditioning. I find either explanation sadder than, for instance, the general Indian inability to tell fact from fiction.

Travelling west from Calcutta, we are going through the burning plains of summer, the thirsty earth scorched brown, waiting for the monsoon rains.

The towns we stop in are uninteresting, places rarely seen by foreign tourists – Sambalpur, the most westerly town of Orissa; Raipur, said to be the hottest city in India; Nagpur, where we find a spanking new hotel in which we would have liked to stay, but it does not open until the following day. April, the spectacularly pretty young receptionist invites us to the official opening.

'The most important man in the town will perform the ceremony,' she says, by way of an inducement.

Why is he the most important man in town, we ask, is he the Mayor or a Minister?

'No', says April with her ravishing smile, 'he is the richest.'

In the small, ugly town of Durg, a large, fat policeman on a motorbike is riding very slowly in the middle of the fairly empty road. We hoot, with no great insistence by Indian standards. He stays in the middle of the road. Eventually, he moves a little to the left. Nat tries to squeeze past. The policeman changes his mind and comes out again. We just touch the rear of his motor-bike. He swerves all over the road, but just manages not to fall.

We stop. The policeman comes, puts his suffused, fat face into Nat's and tells us to follow him. At the police station it turns out that he is the Chief of Police in Durg.

Nat apologises in that awful way that one must to such

turkeycocks of officials. The policeman plays his part to the hilt. He will make a big case of it, he says. He will keep us there for three days at least, maybe more if prison is involved.

After half an hour of this, a man in a yellow shirt, who happens to be there for no reason that we can see, as people always are in India, draws Nat aside. He thinks the affair can be settled here and now. A matter of, shall we say, £4?

We paid and drove away, feeling relieved but ashamed – the giving of bribes being almost as demeaning to the donor as it should be to the receiver.

The twisting road up to Pachmari is punctuated by warning signs, some of them rhyming after a fashion:

'Overtakers make jobs for undertakers.'

'Dangerous curves needs dextrous nerves.'

'On the right is valley side, a little wobble may mean suicide.'

The plateau on which this hill station sits was not found by the British until 1862, when a young captain of the Lancers, J. Forsyth, was sent to explore the Satpura forests which, in those days, were in what were known as the Central Provinces.

He found, at an elevation of 3,500 feet, a saucer-shaped area of about twelve square miles, much of it, he wrote, 'covered in short, green grass, and studded with magnificent trees ... the dark green harra, the arboreous jamun and the common mango dotted the plain in fine clumps, and altogether the aspect of the plateau was much more that of an English park than of any scene I had before come across in India.'

All the water that gathers in the middle of the plateau escapes finally over its edge in pretty cascades. The surrounding country is made up of huge crags of red, sandstone rock. In between the peaks are valleys and deep ravines filled with lush vegetation, some narrow clefts dropping a thousand feet or more.

It is a land of secret gorges, caverns and deep caves, coloured in the local imagination by tales of mythical serpents and vengeful gods.

Scattered among the ravines and canyons are caves decorated with prehistoric paintings, showing hunters with bows and arrows; warriors fighting, some with swords and shields; what appears to be a peace treaty and some domestic scenes of cattle herding and many representations of mothers and motherhood. No-one seems much interested in these.

The wildness of this range of hills may be judged by the fact that the British, with their passion for surveying and mapping, did not discover one ravine until the 1920s. Patal Kot, as it is called, was so hidden that the five hundred or more people who lived there had no contact whatever with anyone else. The lost inhabitants turned out to be descended from the remnants of the Maharatha army, routed by the invading Moghuls centuries ago. They had taken refuge here and had never again emerged. They spoke mostly Maharathi. Not surprisingly, because of their intermarrying, they were prone to hereditary defects.

The British promptly built them a Post Office. It did not prosper. The inhabitants, even if they had known how to write, knew no-one to write to, and there was equally no-one to write to them. In the thirties, more sensibly, they built them a school. Even so, it was not until the 1940s that the people of Patal Kot started to venture into the outside world.

Very soon after Captain Forsyth's discovery of the cool plateau of Pachmarhi, the British acquired it as a sanatorium for their soldiers. Not much later, they developed it as an Army post and eventually as the summer capital of the Central Provinces.

The old graveyard, like others of its kind all over India, tells grim stories of hazards for the Europeans in India in the last century. So many young wives carried off by strange diseases, childbirth and probably heartbreak. Worst of all, the children, twins of two months dead within four days of each other and, as late as 1943, the stark grave of an English boy of three. Poor Surgeon-Major Richard Jackson, aged 41, died in September 1883, 'from the effect of Hornet stings.' Only the Sisters in the Convent of St Joseph lived to a ripe old age, their gravestones recording with pride fifty or sixty years of profession of their faith. One lived to be more than a hundred and another triple grave speaks of three actual sisters, in the secular sense as well as the religious one, who all lived well into their seventies.

But the soldiers of the British Indian Army and their counterparts in the Civil Service were made of stern stuff. They carried on, created a golf course and even a race course. They built a hospital that is still in use, and dotted the place with pretty bungalows, with roofs of curved tiles, and believed that they were fulfilling their rightful destiny.

After Independence, the Indians maintained the military establishments but, as a result of the reorganisation of the old Central Provinces into separate states, Pachmarhi, which now lies in Madhya Pradesh, lost all governmental significance and apart from the military cantonment, comes under the jurisdiction of Hoshangabad.

In very recent years, this enchanted plateau has become the holiday resort of the middle and lower-middle classes of the large towns of the region – Bhopal, Jabalpur, Nagpur, Indore or even further afield, for Indians think nothing of a twelve or fifteen-hour journey.

They come for three or four days and drive around with the boot of their cars open, music blaring at full volume or they hire speeding, hooting jeeps and rush from beauty spot to tourist viewpoint, from the waterfalls to the bathing pools, making as much noise as possible.

This prompts in me speculation about the evident need in Indians for an unending racket. The real India moves so silently, the people with their bare feet, the cattle with soft hooves on dusty roads. The wheels of the bullock carts creak, but it is a timeless friendly sound. Is it too facile to think that this is why the Indians love noise so much, radios shrieking, horns howling, a man sitting alone in a hotel bedroom having the television on at such volume that you can hear every word three rooms away? Are they making up for centuries of oppressive quiet?

Despite the hordes of noisy trippers, it is still perfectly possible to wander in solitary peace through those same grassy glades of short-cropped grass, dotted with magnificent trees that Forsyth spoke of. The jamuns, at this time of year, are dropping their large black berries in a luscious spread upon the ground, and the koels, a kind of cuckoo, announce with a monotonous, repeated call that the mangos are ripe.

One can scramble, too, through the surrounding forests with the faint chance, in evening time, of seeing bison, panthers, bears, jackals, wild boar and even, so they say, a very occasional tiger. And as the gloaming deepens, there is the certainty of jumping out of one's skin as a peacock lets out its demented shriek from the tree above.

Moreover, there can be few experiences more inspiring than to gain the top of Dupgarh, the highest peak of the range, in time to watch the sun set and to see the colour of the far-stretching hills change from sombre green to a lambent violet and purple and to watch the grey-blue sky melt gently to a soft lilac and then to an almost alarming blood red, before settling for a purple glow to match the darkening hills.

It does not take long in an Indian village to get involved in the daily round of events. The essential Indian lack of reticence soon makes one privy to the affairs of everyone, to the feuds and squabbles, to the merits and disgraces of the *dramatis personae*.

Pachmarhi, it is true, is not an average village because it has a rapid turnover of tourists, who come for two or three days and then disappear. They provide an income for the community and push up the prices for everyone else, but do not otherwise impinge on the lives of the inhabitants.

When we arrived, our car broke down outside the photography shop. Moiz Fazal Abbas, the photographer, came from behind his counter, offered cold drinks, and said he would find us a place to stay.

Moiz led us to a modest, modern bungalow, belonging to a Mrs Devasher. On the way, he told us that her husband, a retired Colonel, had died last October. Then, in February, her eldest son, a merchant navy officer, died in Bombay. He stepped into the open door of a lift without looking. The lift was not there. The fall to the bottom of the shaft killed him. What is it, I wondered, about the lives of Indians that they are so often riddled with disaster? The cobra always strikes twice, they say.

Mrs Devasher is a twinkly old lady of seventy-four, with a mischievous sense of humour. Her laugh, which comes brightly at the end of many a teasing sentence takes literally the form of 'Ah-ha-ha.'

She bears her bereavements, her loneliness, her arthritis and the worries of her pacemaker with fortitude. 'One must take what God gives one, isn't it? But I think He has been a little hard on me lately, I don't know why, do you? Ah-ha-ha.'

Mata-ji, as we have learned to call her, is a Roman Catholic though her acceptance of misfortune might well have been inspired by a more fatalistic faith. She let us a rather small room in her house and fussed over us in a grandmotherly way. Unfortunately, I need more space to work, so we continue our search and thus we have fallen in with Mr Torry.

Torry owns two houses and is prepared to let us the empty one or part of his own. He suggests that we take the empty one and furnish it a bit. When we leave in a month's time, he will buy the furniture from us for half what we pay for it. This does not strike me as a very good deal. Nor do I much care for the idea of sharing his house. Torry is a rather morose and hypochondriacal figure, full of grave warnings about everything. We must be very watchful of pickpockets, take care where we walk after dark. The local garage, he says, are crooks, the restaurants dirty. Pachmarhi has gone to the dogs. Nonetheless, he seems kind and, hearing that we are short of money and have to go to Bhopal to a bank, has advanced us some until we can make the tedious journey.

On our second morning in Mata-ji's house, there

appeared a large man with hippy-length hair. He said he was called Sherma and that he had come because he had heard about my son, Nat. He thought that Nat was perhaps a re-incarnation of an Indian hero, Shwara, who cared so lovingly for his father, the Hindu equivalent of pious Aeneas. No Indian son nowadays, he maintained, would look after his father in the way that Nat looks after me.

Sherma was an army photographer, but he took early retirement in order to live on his farm in the forest and to follow the occult sciences and to teach them. He showed us postcards from Europeans who, he said, were his pupils.

He offered to cure me, but on hearing that I had had muscular dystrophy since childhood, decided that it was too late for his magic to work. Against that, he could read the future and claimed that he had warned Mata-ji's son not to go to Bombay, as he would never return. He wanted to tell Nat's fortune, an offer that Nat declined.

Sherma went on to describe his prowess in various fields. He spoke of his affinity with animals that must match Dr Doolittle's, and he invited us to visit him on his farm. He must have concluded that after all Nat was no reborn saint, for we have never heard from him again.

Later Mata-ji told me that it was all nonsense. Sherma had told her son that he must beware of water, which the son dismissed as absurd, on the grounds that he had been going to sea for fifteen years and no harm had yet come to him.

'You cannot tell a person who loves his job to give it up, isn't it? They are all rogues these astrologers, and I tell him so, so he doesn't come to see me. Ah-ha-ha.'

But it was Sherma who said that morning that Torry is a crook, relating tales of property deals that sounded more like shrewd business rather than skullduggery. Yet Mata-ji seems to concur with his opinion though, in her Christian way, she would never express it so firmly.

When we are not house-hunting, we spend our days exploring the countryside round Pachmarhi, seeking out the waterfalls and viewpoints, most of which have English names – Lady Robertson's view, Crump's Crag, Lord Lansdowne's point, even Bishop's Squeeze, which does not commemorate some ecclesiastical indiscretion, but is a narrow gorge admired by a Bishop of Nagpur that is tricky to negotiate and positively dangerous if there is any chance of rain.

Some of these beauty spots have odd or sorry associations. Ladey's point, which most locals take to mean a place where the English ladies used to look at the view, actually records the fate of poor Corporal Ladey who, with two other NCOs after an evening's boozing, went to see the view by moonlight and fell over the edge of the precipice.

Drink played its part, too, at Morton's Leap. Handi Koh is a deep narrow canyon. The story goes that Morton, a young lieutenant stationed here in the twenties, made a drunken bet with a fellow officer that he could leap, in the style of Evil Knievel, over this gorge on his motor-bike. He raced at full speed over the edge, failed to reach the other side and lost both his bet and his life.

I have my doubts about this tale since discovering in the cemetery a grave of Lieutenant Sydney Merriman who, in

1921, 'losing his way in a thick fog rode a bicycle over the precipitous scarp at Handi Koh.'

The pleasures of these excursions are inexhaustible and the beauty of the hills seductive. I could imagine buying a house here, a pretty bungalow, like the late Mrs Wightman's, but I fear the tourists will multiply and the already scarred enchantment vanish entirely.

Pachmarhi is not much of a place for the practicalities of life. There is one place from which one may telephone to the world outside. It is a small shop premises in the middle of the village and it advertises a 24-hour service. For a week its green door was padlocked and a notice said that the line was not working.

Now it is open again and I go and sit in the cramped little room with five or six other optimists and wait for a call to Calcutta. It is hot. There is a fan and sometimes it works but, if by any chance someone gets through on the telephone, the operator switches the fan off to increase the chances of being able to hear. These are in any case slight, because the shop is open to the road at just the place where tourist jeeps sit revving their engines and hooting to attract customers.

There is a bank and the manager, Mr Thakur, is a most obliging person, but the facilities of the bank are limited. So we had to go to Bhopal to get some money, a journey of seven hours each way at the best of times.

The news that we were going soon spread. Moiz the photographer, who was the first person we met in Pachmari asked if we would take his father with us. A cousin had died in Bhopal and the old man wanted to go to pay his respects. Of course we agreed, but then it turned out that three large aunts were going to come as well. My car, which boils over every twenty miles in this heat would never make it with seven passengers. Then Mr Torry wanted to come. He had some business to do in Bhopal, but he cried off as he felt too ill. Several others proposed joining us. In the end, feeling rather guilty and inhospitable, we set off alone.

We went down the twisting road to the plain, 'using dextrous nerves for the dangerous curves' and avoiding wobbles that 'may mean suicide'.

Pachmarhi this year, according to the locals, is hotter than it has ever been. Deforestation has had a disastrous effect on the climate of this place, where only twenty years ago, it was thought of as a 'no-fan station', and people often needed a woolly in the evening even in summer. But 2,500 feet lower the heat was unbearable.

The road ran through farmland of no great interest at this time of year before the coming of the rains, though colourful families in creaking bullock carts brightened the journey for us. At one point not far from Bhopal, we passed through some jungly hills, a wild area of parched woodland. Unknown to us, a hideous tragedy was at that moment unfolding in this lost place.

Bhopal today is most famous for the Union Carbide disaster of 1984 that killed more than 1,000 people and destroyed the health of many thousands more. But it is, in fact, an ancient city, dating from at least the eleventh century and it boasts a fine fort, several palaces, pretty lakes and gardens and what is claimed to be the largest mosque in India.

Nevertheless, it is hard to forget the disaster, for there

is hardly a person who has not got a relation or a friend affected by the poisoning fumes that engulfed the city. The case is still not settled and the victims wait for compensation. For many it will come too late.

The temperature in Bhopal was about 113F, it was also the most difficult city I have ever known in which to find one's way about, so we did our banking as quickly as possible and left again for Pachmari feeling depressed. Our melancholy was compounded by reading in the newspaper of the death of five young children.

They were members of two families of bonded labourers working for a contractor with a stone crushing plant. Bonded labour is nominally illegal. Nonetheless, it is still quite common. The employer, Melumal Kukareja, had employed fourteen tribals for more than a year and had paid them a total of only £50 between them in all that time. When they protested, he beat them. The children were made to work day and night and were treated with great brutality. One of the husbands of the two families had managed to escape, after which the employer redoubled his brutalities. The two mothers, driven to desperation, gathered up their children and fled in the night to the forests through which we had driven.

They lost their way and for two days they wandered, without food or water in the appalling heat. Eventually the children collapsed. The mothers separated and went to search for help. One of them eventually managed to find her way to a village. When help came, five of the children were dead. Two of them were ten years old. Two were eight and the fifth was only two.

The scandal was made worse by the fact that the two

families had complained to the district administration, but nothing was done beyond a mild request to Kukareja to release the two families. He refused, but nobody cared. He had the protection of powerful families.

The fact is that local governments are themselves responsible for employing child labour. As we drove back, I noticed among the road workers, as I have often noticed before, boys and girls, no more than eight years old, humping heavy loads of stone and gravel. It made the enormity of official indifference even more distressing.

Yet, all over India, children work and it is a pattern that is hard to break when, in grinding poverty, the few rupees a child may bring home can make all the difference between the family's having something to eat rather than nothing.

We have found perfect lodgings in the house of a retired commander of the Pachmari military centre. Brigadier Dwivedi is a man of propriety and exactitude. He also has a considerate nature that one does not necessarily associate with army training. The three-roomed apartment that he has let to us has four steep steps to the entrance. He has had built a concrete ramp, so that I can fizz in and out in my electric chair without help.

The Brigadier once had ideas of starting a safari lodge nearby in the forests, but he lost heart as there was little encouragement from the State government. He settled instead for building three cottages on his plot of land to let to tourists. He receives them all with punctilious courtesy and otherwise spends his time tending his garden.

Mrs. Dwivedi, a slightly severe but good-looking lady, is a doctor specialising in obstetrics, and she works in the local family-planning department.

Opposite the gate into the compound is a training school for military bands, called Cariappa after India's first post-Independence Commander-in-Chief. We are woken each morning by bugles tooting a Reveille, which is reasonable enough, but there follows every known bugle call – Come to the Cookhouse Door, Boys, Beating the Retreat, the Last Post, what sounds like blasts of Triumph and Victory, all in random order – calculated to induce a severe case of schizophrenia in anyone of a military obedience.

Many of the Brigadier's paying guests are intrigued by my wheelchair and, with typical Indian inquisitiveness, want to know what is the matter with me, how much my chair costs and, with a measure of obliquity, how I managed to conceive five children. I rather enjoy these visits, particularly one from a Nagpur journalist, who normally specialises in environmental questions, and who knocked on the door and said, 'I hope I am not disturbing you, Mr. Chase.' It seems that he had been told in the village that James Hadley Chase was staying at Lake View and that, although this did not immediately appear to be a 'green' issue, it was his duty to investigate. Such is the nature of Indian gossip, which weaves in instant myth and fantasy.

The Brigadier, with his usual concern, tells me that I should not receive just anyone who comes knocking at the door. He says he has no wish, as it were, to censor my visitors, but he feels I am being imposed upon. I tell him that I like these makers of polypropylene from Indore or bank officials, who say that if I do not stay with them when I come to Ahmedabad, they will never raise their heads again. Shashi has brought this question of callers to a head.

Shashi is a boy of nervous energy. He tells me he is fifteen, though he looks older. His father, a friend of the Brigadier's, is a forestry expert and was once in charge of the nearby Sapura national park. He came into my sitting-room to ask if I had any stamps for his collection.

He appears to be an avid collector with eclectic tastes, liking pencils, bottles, coins and other oddments. He is somehow not like other Indian boys of his age, being less deferential and more direct in expressing his opinions.

When I mentioned that we had been to Bhopal, he wanted to know whether we had visited the palace. He asked if I knew about the stone that the old Nawabs of Bhopal once owned.

'If it touched iron, it turned it immediately into gold. The stone disappeared. But one day, in the British time, an elephant which had an iron ring on its tusk was wallowing in the lake and must have touched the stone with its tusk, because when it came out of the water, the iron ring had turned to gold. The British drained the lake three times searching for the stone, but they never found it.'

When I asked if he believed this tale, Shashi said, 'Every Indian knows there is a stone that turns iron into gold.'

'But do you believe it?'

'Yes, I do, otherwise how could the elephant's ring have become gold?'

Shashi's beliefs are intractable. Despite my providing him with some stamps and a couple of unusual pencils, he told me a day or two ago that he hates the British. They are enemies of India. Nonetheless, he likes all the British people he has met.

'It is the policies I hate and I would happily fight the British.' He says he has been taught that the British deliberately engineered the partition of India, so that they could 'divide and rule'. It was they who encouraged Jinnah's intransigence.

He is passionate about India. 'My country is now

strong and no longer obsessed by money, which was our downfall. The ingenious British won India, by taking advantage of our weakness for money and our susceptibility to bribes. India was a rich country, but you took all our wealth.'

On the whole, Shashi's arguments are well marshalled, if somewhat misinformed, and he expresses them vehemently. He certainly knows more about the history of his country than his equivalent at home would know about British history. And I admire his spirit. On the Partition question, I suggested that he might read *Freedom at Midnight*, as being by neither an Indian nor an Englishman.

'My father has it, but it looks a bit long.' Nevertheless, he said he would try.

Intrigued as to whether these views were really taught in Indian schools, I related the discussion to the Brigadier. The result was explosive. The Brigadier, normally so urbane, treated me to a tirade. The boy, he said, was subnormal. 'He is seventeen and he is still in tenth grade. He cannot pass any examinations. Really he is mentally retarded. You must ignore everything he said. Leave all memory of him behind in India. I know our textbooks and they do not teach that. Other young people would never say such things.'

The Brigadier went on in this vein for a long time. Moments after he left me, he came rushing back. One of the military bands was in full Om-pom-pom just outside the gate.

'You hear that tune?', demanded the Brigadier. 'It was written before Independence by a Muslim who chose to go and live in Pakistan. We have had our troubles with

Pakistan, but that does not mean that we ignore a good tune. We play it and it is a famous air, known to all Indians.' He asked the boy who looks after me to confirm this, which he did.

I cannot decide whether the Brigadier's agitation was inspired more by his anxiety to dispel a false impression or by a wish to erase from my mind what he assumed I would regard as an unforgivable discourtesy.

Perhaps it was as well that Shashi was to leave soon, as I, in my turn, did not want to offend the Brigadier by continuing to entertain Shashi. Luckily, he did not go before he had shed an eerie light on the murder of poor Mrs Wightman.

All the bungalows in Pachmarhi have gates across the drive to keep out the buffaloes and cows that wander free around the roads. Sometimes one beast, more ingenious than its fellows, learns how to lift the catch and pushes open the gate. Then it will feast on the carefully tended flowers and shrubs until a furious gardener, shrieking tribal oaths, rushes at it brandishing a stick, and there follows a lively chase during which the creature's trampling hooves will do even more damage than its placid munching.

Mrs Wightman's house lies some five hundred yards beyond where Mr Torry now lives alone, estranged from his son and daughters, who lead their own lives. The gate at the end of her drive is difficult to open. A tangle of briar has closed it more securely than any catch. Beyond, one can see the remains of what was a beautiful garden, filled with more unusual plants that most of the gardens of Pachmarhi. Weeds scramble over what were once flower beds. Bougainvillea runs wild over unexpected cacti. No-one has cared for this very English place for ten years or more, not since Mrs Wightman was murdered.

She had been married to an English businessman. When he retired, they settled happily in Pachmarhi rather than going back to England and, after his death, she stayed on. Mrs Wightman was popular. She led a quiet life, spending much time with another English widow, who fled in misery after her murder. She was a good friend and used to call on Mata-ji very frequently when the Colonel was ill. No-one could possibly have borne her any ill will. Yet one night she was hacked to death and her servant found her in a pool of blood in the morning.

The case has never been solved, but the old inhabitants say they know who did it. Or, if he did not do it himself, who arranged it.

This man was seen walking near Mrs Wightman's house late that night. And who in Pachmarhi ever walks out late at night? There used to be no question of doing so, because of the danger from wild animals, and the habit of being indoors early still lingers, at any rate from the old-timers.

There were some documents to do with her finances, so rumour has it, sitting on her desk, awaiting signature. Was she killed because she would not sign?

If ever Mrs Wightman's name is mentioned to this man, they say, he turns pale and his hands tremble uncontrollably. I have not yet managed to try this out to judge whether it is true.

My young friend Shashi says that last year he went into Mrs Wightman's house with a couple of friends. They picked a moment when the police guards, who have watched over the place ever since the murder, were absent. It was quite easy to get in and rather eerie, as nothing had been moved. Apart from the dust, it felt as if Mrs Wightman had just gone out for a while. Her driving licence and her husband's licence were both lying on a table. Shashi admired their very English china, which he thought pretty, and even more the silver pheasants that sat on the dining-table.

'Do you believe in ghosts?', Shashi once asked me. I was rather non-committal, as I wanted to know what was coming.

'You see, we were very frightened that the police might catch us in the house and think that we had something to do with the case. That night I dreamt that I was going towards the house and, when I was getting near the door, I looked up and there in a tree was a big black dog, lying across a branch. It was dead and blood dripped from its neck.'

'Then, in my dream, I was caught by the police and I woke up, very afraid. The next day I learned that Mrs Wightman had had a big black dog and that the murderer had killed it and thrown it up into the tree.'

Shashi had no definite views about who had killed Mrs Wightman, but supposed erroneously that it was her servant. He was right, however, in believing that she had a big black dog which, according to Mata-ji, was found locked up in the kitchen on the morning after her death.

This year, Shashi went back to look at the house. There was no guard, but the house was empty – no pretty china, no silver pheasants. He maintained, and everyone agreed with this view, that the police supposedly guarding the house had stolen everything.

I went to look, pushing aside the tangled briar, and found easily a way into the house. It was a scene of sad dereliction. A few odd bits of solid furniture lay about, but nothing of value. Papers were strewn about the floor of what had plainly been the living-room, among them photographs of Mrs Wightman and her husband on holiday, a pleasant-looking couple, manifestly deserving of a happier end.

The house rots. It is for sale, but no-one will buy it with its gruesome associations. I was a little tempted myself, as it would be a delight to restore the garden, but Pachmarhi has declined in recent years and perhaps I, too, like Shashi might come to believe in ghosts.

We left Pachmarhi with regrets of various kinds. Parting from Mata-ji was painful. We had visited her every day and she had come to expect us. She now feared that she would never see us again and she wept. We had not managed to see a leopard or a bison. And we had not solved the mystery of Mrs Wightman's murder. Moreover, it had become cooler there, although the rains are at least three weeks late, and we have now plunged into the heat of the plains.

Against that, it was exciting to be on the road again, with the prospect of many things to see. In the slightly cooler weather, the car did not boil over and I was glad that the rains were late, as I knew that the windscreen on my side leaked and that my wiper did not work.

We have reached our first objective – Khajuraho. Here, we roam among the quantities of temples that are scattered in and around the small town. They are among the most famous in India, largely because of the elaborate and detailed erotic carvings that cover both the outsides and the interiors of these buildings. It is, in some ways, quite wrong that the fame of these temples should stem from their pornographic potential. As pieces of architecture, as examples of building genius and as works of decorative artistry, they are unsurpassed anywhere in India.

The builders, known as the Chandelas, belonged to a Rajput dynasty that reached its peak in the tenth and eleventh centuries. They built in the most extraordinary manner, assembling all the pieces of stone beforehand, cutting them and carving them according to a plan and then putting them all together, without mortar, but with an interlocking system like a three-dimensional jigsaw – an almost incredible feat considering that the main towers of some of the temples are more than 100 feet high.

The carvings themselves are supreme works of art, depicting warriors and horsemen, animals and gods but, above all, women. Beautiful women, many of them dancers, but otherwise girls going about their everyday lives – this one washing her hair, the next one taking a thorn out of her foot, another one yawning sleepily, still others gossiping, playing, stroking themselves in a suggestive manner, or just looking seductive. In each case, the detail is remarkable, the drops of water from the wet hair, the mark where the thorn was, the mosquito bite that needed scratching, the stimulated nipple – all minutely delineated.

Yet one cannot escape the fact that the emphasis is on sex. So many of the girls are portrayed in the act of making love. Everywhere, couples are entwined in embraces and positions that challenge the imagination. Can one really do that, one wonders?

More, one speculates on what prompted this effusion of sexual activity, sculpted with such painstaking exactitude. Some argue that the carvers were merely representing every aspect of life and that lovemaking is just as much a part of human existence as war, dancing, growing crops, even hair-washing or scratching a mosquito bite. Others maintain that life at the time of the Chandela dynasty was a bawdy affair, free from prudery and prim Western notions, even that sex was a pathway to enlightenment.

The second theory seems to me more likely, especially after looking at a frieze which, as one guidebook says with some delicacy, shows that a horse can be a person's best friend. Against that, most of the sculptures deal with healthy, normal, if hyperactive sex.

Sexuality, like everything else in India, defies any certainties. So much of the Hindu religion is concerned with sex. The lingam of the god Shiva is the object of regular worship in many temples. The Kama Sutra must be the world's best known sex manual. In the fort at Gwalior, there is a temple built by one Maharajah where he and his new bride retired for lessons in lovemaking. In Jaipur, there is a house where the young nobles used to go to school to learn the etiquette of sex.

Even today, it is quite usual for a young bride's mother-in-law to present the girl with a book full of the most startling pictures showing what she should do to amuse her husband. Nudity is abhorred, yet one day we passed a young man standing by the side of the road quite openly masturbating, for all to see. Practitioners of yoga train themselves to astonishing feats of unusual strength, such as carrying a suitcase on an erect penis. The late Rajneesh was not alone among gurus in promoting sexual frolics among his devotees.

How does all this equate with the prudery and modesty of everyday life? Virginity is absolutely essential for any girl looking for a husband. There is, of course, a double standard as far as the men are concerned. Traditionally, a young man is taken to a brothel to make up for the lack of any sexual possibilities among the young women he may meet.

It seems to me that there is a further double standard in the Indian attitude to sex. Everyone is perpetually aware of the powerful undercurrent of sexuality, which manifests itself in the androgyne of the hand-holding men and the provocativeness of the women, but no-one ever speaks of it. A great deal happens, but everyone pretends that it doesn't. An attitude, I suppose, not so very different from that which prevails among British politicians.

As we travel north from Khajuraho, it seems to me that there is a wholly different feeling in the air. It is not so much a question of the landscape. We have, it is true, left the wildness of the teak forests and the rushing streams of the country in which the temples lay. The survival of the tenth-century temples is due, in fact, to the remote hills that deterred the Moghuls from discovering and surely destroying them. But once we lunched at the little-known town of Orchha and we were at once aware of a complete cultural change.

Orchha is a perfect, if decaying, medieval Rajput town, far removed in spirit from Khajuraho, because at least one Maharaja came to an easy accommodation with the Moghul emperor, building an enormous palace for a visit by Jehangir. We stayed, like him, for only an hour or two, but it was a place of civilised, albeit faded, beauty.

We are now plunged into the tourist circuit, fortunate in being out of season and doubly lucky in that the monsoon, which should be in full flood, is late this year. We roamed the fort and palace of Gwalior in comparative solitude and, even at Agra found that it was possible to view the Taj Mahal in reasonable peace.

When in Agra, I like to go to see how the Dayal Bagh,

or Holy Samadh of the Radhasoami Faith, is progressing. This must be one of the most extraordinary building enterprises going forward anywhere in the world. It is a large temple built of marble which, when it is finished, will be quite as big as the Taj Mahal.

The founder of the Radhasoami Faith, Shiv Dayal Singh, was born in 1818 and claimed to be an incarnation of the Supreme Creator. The doctrines that he propounded are appealing. His religion was to be open to all peoples, regardless of caste, creed or nationality. There were no formal rites or ceremonies. In principle, it is, according to a modern account, 'based upon purely scientific grounds and nothing is accepted that cannot be supported by facts, i.e. working of natural laws and phenomena as observed in this world. Nothing is to be believed on hearsay or as blind faith.'

If one pursues the question, it proves not to be quite so simple, requiring considerable suspension of disbelief and certainly acceptance of the transmigration of souls. Nonetheless, the building, in which the ashes of the founder are enshrined, is informed by an agreeably ecumenical spirit.

Shiv Dayal Singh died in 1878, but the grandiose scheme for his memorial was not started until 1904. It has been building ever since. So far, it has reached only the second storey, rising somewhere between forty and sixty feet, but the plan is for a huge, double, onion dome topped by a pinnacle, reaching in all to 195 feet and surrounded by minarets of 104 feet.

The architectural style is a jumble, incorporating Hindu, Muslim and Christian features, so that one doorway may combine Indian, Moghul and Gothic shapes in its arch.

The decoration is immensely elaborate, the carving of one pillar often taking two years or more to complete. I used to think that the designs, set as they were in the early years of this century, were too sugary and sentimental but, as the building grows, I find them more attractive and unquestionably impressive in the quality of the workmanship. The pietra dura is as fine as much of the inlay work to be seen in the Taj Mahal; the carving is often equally skilful.

Work goes on all day beside the building. Some hundred masons and craftsmen are employed for wages of probably less than £10 a month, yet many of them have worked for their whole lifetime on this site. Several of the younger workers are the children of older ones.

Progress is slow. The Holy Samadh has now been building for eighty years, and will certainly take another forty to finish. The Taj Mahal took only twenty-one years to build, but there were 20,000 workers to do it. At least their modern successors need have no fear that they might share the fate of their forebears. Legend has it that all those who worked on Mumtaz's mausoleum had their right hands cut off and the architect had his eyes put out, lest any of them should ever attempt to create a comparable monument. I fear that the Holy Samadh will never match the beauty of the Taj, but I find it wonderful that such craftsmanship is still practised.

This last grateful observation is inspired to some extent by a growing horror at the appalling ugliness of modern Indian taste. As we drive along, we see by the side of the road examples of architecture, particularly new villas, that make us laugh out loud. Yesterday, not long after leaving the forlorn splendour of the deserted city of Fatehpur Sikri, built by Akbar, I noticed a monstrous, new house, the front of which was divided into squares that looked like giant condom packets.

It is not just a question of buildings. In almost every hotel all over the country, from the humblest lodging-house up to even the grandest hotel chains, one sees a singularly offensive make of pottery. It has a greyish-yellow colour, streaked with smudges of brown, so that it looks as if someone has forgotten to wash it up.

How is it, one wonders, that a people who, over the centuries, have produced such glories as the temples of Khajuraho, the palaces of the Rajputs, the monuments of the Moghuls and every kind of exquisite carving, bronze, jewel, fresco, miniature, silk, cloth and all the rest, can today produce and supposedly admire such dross?

The same is true to a lesser degree of Italy. There the legacy of the Romans and the Renaissance is betrayed by the ghastliness of so much modern design.

I had been puzzled, since we reached touristland, to find how large a proportion of the foreigners is Italian. Now I reflect how much the Italians and the Indians have in common.

They are both what one might call clustering nations. With the exception of the people of Coorg, the Indians prefer to live cheek by jowl in villages and walk out to work in the fields, as do the Italians – as opposed to the British who like to live as far as possible from one another in cottages scattered over the land.

They both live the greater part of their lives in the street and there enjoy the maximum amount of noise. Even after six months in India, I cannot believe that the inhabitants of a village can bear the shrieking of a radio played at such volume that it is unbearable to me half a mile away.

Both Indians and Italians talk at a yelling pitch, so that one feels that any conversation must be a furious row, yet it ends in unexpected amity.

As a final thought on taste, it has often struck me as peculiar that so highly developed and ancient a society should have such an affection for glitter and tinsel, which I would have thought was a primitive predilection. But here in Rajasthan, I have a different perception. Grumbling as I have been about the garish paint on the modern temples, I look with pleasure at the Rajasthani women working in the fields, the brilliant colours of their saris and the glinting of the gold threads in their headdresses bringing life to a bland desert landscape.

I once lived in Jaipur for six months, writing a biography of the last Maharaja and I loved it. Now I am wondering whether, in my search for somewhere to settle, the familiar city with old friends might not be the answer.

It is a problem of our times that change comes so rapidly to trample on our memories. When I was here before, people used to tell me how marvellous Jaipur had been in the old days. Looking at the 1940s photograph taken by Cecil Beaton of orderly street scenes in an immaculate town, uniformly pink and spotlessly clean, I could imagine what they were talking about, but I was so delighted by the adventure of learning about the Rajputs and their history, by the beauty of the palaces and by the strangeness of India that it seemed unimportant. Jaipur was to me as entrancing as Florence had been many years before and about which people had said exactly the same things.

In the eight years since I was there, the decline has accelerated. It is now my turn to grumble that things are not what they used to be. The population has increased to nearly insupportable levels, with people sleeping on the pavements not far from the centre. The dirt has multiplied, many of the pink buildings look grey-brown, and new developments have robbed the suburbs of much open space.

On a more personal level, I find some awkwardness. Some of the older, grand nobles of the court did not like my life of Maharaja Man Singh. It was not critical of him, but nothing less than a panegyric would have satisfied Rajput pride, which is more concerned with myths of glory than with academic truth.

Then, too, the royal family of Jaipur has been riven by a family feud, now happily somewhat abated, which as I like all the parties involved, I find sad. It bears out, however, one of the side issues of my book that caused annoyance. I pointed up the quarrelsome nature of the Indian princely families, especially the Rajputs. Yet even today, when they are stripped of their titles and their power, the royal families of Gwalior, Udaipur and Jaipur are not alone in managing to conduct family disputes in public.

I have decided that Jaipur, for all its historic interest and aesthetic charms and despite the welcome from various old friends, is not where I want to live. The cities and even the smaller towns of India are made oppressive by the intractable chaos, the sheer mass of people crushed into too small an area, the noise, the traffic, the dirt, the fear that all these and the lives of the people can only get worse. As this journey goes on, I come more and more to think that if I am to stay in India it must be in the countryside – the wilder the better.

So I have come back to Calcutta to see my old friend, Basant Dube, on whose tea estate in Orissa we stayed in May. At that time, Basant had waxed lyrical about a project he had long in mind and in which he invited me to join.

Some five or six hours south of Calcutta is a beautiful

National Park called Simlipal. It is comparatively little visited, because of its remoteness and because there are few places for people to stay either inside the park or nearby, yet it is one of the most exciting parks in India.

It covers nearly 3,000 square kilometres of hilly country, much of it covered with forests of Sal trees. There are pretty rivers and some spectacular waterfalls. The park is full of wild life – tigers, leopards, elephants, bison, sloth bears, spotted and barking deer. The birds, too, are exceptional in their abundance. The local inhabitants are almost as unusual as the animals, being aboriginal tribal people, in many cases still hunter-gatherers. Mark Sykes in his *Travels with my Elephant* describes a visit to some villagers, who live by gathering honey from the rock bees, being lowered over the cliff edge on lianas and throwing a flame torch into the hollows where the bees nest. Simlipal is a near paradise.

Basant's plan is to build a forty-room hotel on some land beside a lake, not far from one entrance to the park. He hopes to build some cottages within the park in association with the hotel, and to reproduce what is known as the Khairi experiment of breeding tigers in captivity. The place would be attractive to foreigners and also a refuge for people in Calcutta, Bhubaneshwar and various other cities who have few places within reach for a short holiday.

It appeals to me very much as an idea, because it includes the concept of what is now known as eco-tourism, which is to say a form of tourism that aims to preserve the place that is visited rather than destroy it.

During my search for a place to settle, I have been

uneasy that, in my determination to be in the country-side, I may have been deceiving myself as to my capacity for dealing with isolation and loneliness. Here seems to be the perfect solution – something to do that is worth-while doing, a guarantee of company and of people to look after me and being able, with comparative ease to reach Calcutta, my favourite among Indian cities, more friends and much that is civilised. The search is over.

# Epilogue

We flew back to Jaipur, where we had left the car to get the gearbox fixed for the third time and to have the windscreen sealed. Nat had to return to England, so my godson, Luke Geddes, came out to push my wheelchair and to drive.

There were many complications. My visa had nearly run out. I had tried to have it extended by a month in Calcutta, but had been told that it could not be done in any circumstances. It seemed to me that in Jaipur, where I had friends, things would be easier. Moreover, I thought that, if I had a doctor's certificate to say that I was not fit to fly for a month or so, the officials could hardly refuse. I armed myself with such a certificate and went with a friend to see his friend in the immigration office.

This friend of a friend was adamant and mildly cross. Adamant because the rules had been changed and he no longer had the power to grant an extension; cross because the new regulations deprived him and his colleagues of a steady source of bribes from neglectful tourists.

The next problem was the car. The gearbox seemed to work, but the garage had forgotten about the windscreen wipers and had contrived to make a hole in the fuel tank. Eventually we got away, heading for Bombay. On the day we left, the monsoon started in earnest. The windscreen leaked as much as ever and the car could have doubled as a swimming pool. On the next day, the new wiper on my side gave up.

We had planned to spend the night in an old farmhouse belonging to Nahar Singh, the Rawat of Deogarh, one of the nobles of the court of Udaipur. The house lay beside a lake, set among hills that the Rawat said were, geologically speaking, the oldest in the world. The landscape certainly had about it a gloriously lost feeling and the lake swarmed with rare birds. It was a place of romantic beauty. The Rawat and his family were charming.

Owing to the monsoon, all the telephones were out of order, so we had not been able to book one of the three rooms that the Rawat lets to visitors. When we got there, all the rooms were free, but two were inaccessible to me in my wheelchair and in the third the bathroom did not work. We had to press on over terrible roads. The journey seemed ill-starred.

In Udaipur, Luke developed malaria.

With amazing resilience, three days later, Luke decided he was well enough to go on. The roads became much better, but on the smoothest road we had seen since Jaipur, we had a puncture. Luke, brought up in the safety of British tyre regulations, had never changed a wheel. He learned quickly. We drove three miles. Another puncture. We were, of course, twenty miles from the nearest place that could mend a tyre, let alone sell us a new wheel – one of them had crumbled to a disc of rust.

The hotel we wanted to stay in at Ahmedabad had been pulled down, but we found another and a friendly garage.

Two days later we were on our way again, with new tyres and wipers that wiped with vigour.

The monsoon, which had slackened, now fell in lashing strings. After an hour, my wiper blade fell off and Luke's stopped. At a garage, a gormless youth tried for an hour to revive the wiper motor. He failed. An old man crumbled a cigarette over the windscreen. 'You will see with no trouble,' he said. For a while we did, but it was a frightening drive to Surat.

The next day was the last. We had the wipers mended yet again and the rain was light. The traffic, on the other hand, was heavy. The day dragged and, by the time darkness fell, we were still fifty miles from Bombay in a stationary queue of lorries. The road was narrow and on the other side was an equally motionless line going in the opposite direction. The hours crept by. Occasionally, we could advance a little by sneaking down the queue on the inside. On one such venture, we got stuck behind a broken-down hay lorry. Luke tried to reverse. The gearstick would not move – not into any gear. It was 11.30 p.m. A night by the roadside seemed the only possibility.

Two young men appeared and asked what we were doing. We explained. 'We fix, no problem,' they said. For three quarters of an hour they scrabbled about, taking the gearbox to pieces by the light of a torch. Finally it worked, even if a sound like jangling keys came from the gears. The young men thought £4 a generous reward.

We drove on, reaching Bombay at 2.30 a.m. We hunted for the Royal Bombay Yacht Club, where we were to stay. Clear directions were hard to come by. We knew it was near the Gateway of India. Luke drove right up to this imperial monument. The police arrested him. He refused with such majestic indignation to pay the bribe they demanded that they let him go.

I relate this catalogue of aggravations in order to illustrate how frustrating everyday life in India can be. In some ways, the irritations were beginning to undermine my decision.

Against that, while nearly everything in India is difficult, almost nothing is impossible if you know the right person. £20 to the police in Bombay sorted out my visa problem. And, after all, where else in the world will two good-natured people appear from nowhere in the middle of the night to repair a gearbox? There is unquestionably something about India that captures one's affections forever.

A large part of one floor of the Royal Bombay Yacht Club is occupied by the Irish Consulate. Mr Callaghan, the Honorary Consul, is a handsome man, the rich complexion of his face crowned by that flowing, silvery hair which distinguished-looking Irishmen are so often blessed with. He is always immaculately dressed and exudes an air of old-fashioned courtesy, enlivened with humour. The Consul has lived in India for thirty-three years and, by some strange and rather grand dispensation from the Indian Government, is called in his passport not, 'Mr Robert W. Leybourne Callaghan', but just 'Callaghan of India'.

Callaghan has earned his living as a business consultant, working much of the time for Hoffman Laroche. No-one knows more about the workings of Indian politics and Indian business. Much of it enrages him, especially the corruption. He explained to me how many civil service jobs could only be got by bribing a minister. (He claimed, by the way, never to have given a bribe in his life. I winced to think of my visa.)

It has been a story that I have heard over and over again. The children of so many of my Indian friends live and work abroad and have no intention of returning. It is not just that they can earn so much more outside India. It is that no matter how talented they are, nor how fine their qualifications, they will never get a job worthy of their skills without both the right connections and a hefty bribe.

Callaghan's disapproval of much that is Indian is balanced by an understanding of their way of thought. He has a theory that the absence of urgency in Indian affairs can be attributed to their sense of time's being coloured by the belief in transmigration of souls. If one is to have another life, then nothing in this one seems to be pressing.

Perhaps because he is Irish and therefore tends towards a harbouring of historical grievances, he believes that the Indians hate Europeans. Yet he chooses to live among them. Callaghan personified the uncertainties that beset me.

I did not believe him on the subject of Indian dislike of Europeans. In Bombay, I talked to so many supposedly Anglophile Indians, notably a businessman, Rozal Mehta, who was educated at Rugby, who not only loved it, but endured the English public school system better than many English boys. His method of dealing with latter day Flashmans was both ingenious and very Indian. He arranged to have a large hamper of delicacies delivered to his fag master at the beginning of each term.

Other people in Bombay unsettled me in a different way. They predicted that, within a few years, the whole of India would split apart, the union breaking up into religious and ethnic fragments.

Then this happened:

By coincidence, Luke's father, Hugh Geddes, happened to be in Bombay. He was anxious to make the journey to Ahmednagar, where he was born when his father was in the army. I was not very interested in this idea. I was born in 27 Welbeck Street in London. I have never given the place a glance and certainly would not expect Hugh to accompany me on a three-day trip to look at it.

It seemed ungracious to refuse, particularly as Luke wanted to go and could not leave me alone. We spent the night in Pune (Poona). In the morning, we set off in a chauffeur-driven car. The driver was not too bad by Indian standards. But, as we came into Ahmednagar, he failed to see a speed-breaker. We went over it at full speed.

Sitting in the back of an Indian car, one is directly over the axle. I flew up in the air and landed with force on the end of my spine. The crack was loud and the pain intense.

The next hours were among the most unpleasant that I can remember. We went to the military hospital – the place where Hugh was born. They could do nothing for a civilian and offered instead the civil hospital or the Booth hospital 'which might be a bit cleaner.' As it was Sunday, it was hard to rouse anyone, but it turned out that Booth meant General Booth and the Salvation Army. Two kindly Americans appeared and soon after some drugs and an X-ray of sorts. Two crushed vertebrae.

We hired an ambulance. This was an old Bedford van

with a narrow shelf and a stretcher made of steel. It took two hours to get back to Pune. The roads had seemed smooth in the morning; now they consisted of brutal potholes. We spent two nights in Pune and hired a luxury ambulance (the shelf was three inches wider) for the six hour journey to Bombay over more serious potholes in the twisting mountain road.

This last experience daunted me and my resolve still wavers. I yearn for those forests of Sal trees, for the waterfalls and the strutting peacocks in the glades of the Simlipal hills. But can I live happily a six-hour Indian ambulance ride from the nearest medical help? I shall wait and see.